Insults May Vary

Snarky Humor for the Huddled Masses

By David Ferrell

This book consists entirely of fictional "writings."

Any other forms of expression purportedly "seen" or imagined on these pages—including, for example, secret codes, lewd anagrams, algebraic equations, or foreign-language furniture assembly instructions—are purely inadvertent and not the intent of the author, unless, of course, they create a wonderful, pleasing effect, in which case I'm impressed that you noticed.

Thank you.

No whales, endangered waterfowl, or Hollywood celebrities were harmed in the writing of this book. As far as I know, George Clooney and Brad Pitt remain friends.

DEDICATED TO THE REMARKABLE FERRELL CLAN:
ALINA, CINDY, AND CLAIRE . . .

AND IN LOVING MEMORY OF SCOTT AND WALT

Table of Contents

A Visitor's Guide to Witt's End	1
Youngfellas: Tales of the Fourth-Grade Mob	6
Table Talk: Of Bonbons and Bon Mots	13
ART REVIEW: A Hard Look at 'Lady Godiva's Belly Button'	20
The Lowdown On Famous Secret Societies	25
A Memory to Savor: The Great Food Fight at Spago	33
A Special Wise Guy: The Advice Guru	39
Insults May Vary: Verbal Attacks for Any Occasion	46
Novel Flops: Unpublished Sequels of the Literary Giants	54
Gobsmacked to a Fair Farthing (and Other Exciting New Cliches)	65
Now It Can Be Told: One Man's Torrid Love Affair With Liz Taylor	73
According to Nostradamus, It's Really All About Me	79
A Genius at Work in Real Time	86
Tour Notes of a Spoken Word Artist	91
Strange Coincidences: Eight Billion People on Earth, and YOU Are the One Reading This!	99
The Mating Dance of Lawyers	105
Lesser Artists of the Renaissance	118

Reviews of My Finest Craft Wines	127
Dr. Cronquist's Final Paper	131
FILM REVIEW: The Sad and Hilarious Brilliance of 'The Elevator'	137
Can This Marriage Endure?	143
So Many Women! Dating a Multiple Personality	150
A Farewell to Yarns: Drafts of My Resignation Letter from the Writers' Group	155
Fight Night in L.A.	160
Acknowledgements	172
Author Bio	173

David Ferrell

A Visitor's Guide to Witt's End

Not every traveler yearns for the sedate charms of Paris or San Francisco. Some bold spirits canoe the steamy, malarial backwaters of the Congo; others trek through the joyless, frozen hell of the Yukon. These days, an ungodly number of Americans are spending whatever free hours they have in the loud, gritty, overcrowded place known as Witt's End—a destination offering the ultimate test of mental fortitude.

"Where joie de vivre goes to die," boasts one popular website. Witt's End is notable for its "full-on sensory bombardment," a fact reflected in its catchy civic motto: "Never relax—not for a single mother-lovin' second." Keep your eyes open, keep your hands on your wallet—great advice in any tourist mecca, but it's especially apt in this melting pot of incinerated dreams, where millions of angry losers live shoehorned into a deep alluvial depression between a rock and a hard place.

You can see and feel the angst—it hangs in the air like a chemical fog. Sporadic offshore breezes, known locally as the Ill Winds, create unpredictable weather patterns marked by oppressive dark clouds and electrical storms. It rains an average of 2.6 inches on every parade.

Thousands of newcomers arrive in Witt's End daily. Most agree they would rather be anywhere else. They discover that the stakes are too high, the rewards are too low, and time is too short. Here, the rigid enforcement of Murphy's Law assures that the disasters you were bracing yourself for are bound to happen—probably sooner than you think.

Up to the challenge? If you go, bring a GPS. It's easy to get lost among the Mountains of Debt that frame the city's south flank, or in the teeming, unincorporated suburbs of Strife, Legal Wrangling, and Utter Burnout. Tourists generally gravitate to Witt's End's vibrant central core—a high-rise, high-rent district populated by a colorful cast of corporate drones, back-stabbers, twitching sociopaths, nervous Nellies, and various other species of trampled-upon working stiff. Dandied up in suits, ties, pricey pumps, and tight skirts, they wear their festering psychological quirks like face paint.

Spotting them is one of the great attractions of Witt's End nightlife. Excellent public viewing places include historic watering holes where the exploited suckers convene nightly to wait out the interminable rush hour. Exorbitant hors d'oeuvres specials are offered at trendy gastropubs such as *H8 My Life*, on Fuckettall Street, and *Payne & Mizry*, on Gotta-B-Abetter Way. Arrive early to see the lightweights sling back their margaritas and Mai Tais, then drunkenly stagger away en route to collecting humiliating and costly DUIs.

Late-evening theatrics vary widely. It's not uncommon to see belligerent sots clash over race, politics, religion, and myriad personal scandals and vendettas. Get lucky, and you may witness that most spectacular aspect of Witt's End bar life: someone completely blowing a head gasket, often leading to a full-on brouhaha.

Fun fact: More inebriated cretins are hauled off to the pokey in Witt's End than in all of Portugal, Yemen, and Mozambique combined.

In defiance of normal metropolitan trends, Witt's End's growth rate has spiked even as unemployment rates have tripled and housing and food costs have shot into the stratosphere.

Rampant crime keeps every decent citizen living on tenterhooks. In a poll, sixty-eight percent of the population expressed paralyzing fear of being shot, mugged, robbed, or punched in the face by a random passing stranger. Fifty percent expected to be verbally assaulted by a hostile spouse or in-law, with most respondents noting that "it has happened before" or "it happens all the time." Thirty-two percent cited a range of other dire concerns, from being tarred and feathered by skinheaded extremists to being lashed to a broken water heater and dropped down an abandoned well. Many feared fear itself: public panic attacks are illegal under a longstanding local ordinance. Misdemeanor cases are punishable by a fine, imprisonment, or both. More serious breakdowns often result in felony convictions and mandatory public floggings that are televised on LookSeeTV, the public-service channel.

Politically, Witt's End is what the League of Women Voters describes as a "hot mess." Last year, an ad hoc advisory committee was formed to investigate tens of thousands of unresolved citizen complaints. In eleven months' time, the committee itself emerged as the No. 1 source of citizen outrage, with several watchdog groups clamoring for felony indictments.

Witt's End is divided by charter into fifteen geographic districts. These heavily gerrymandered fiefdoms are headed up by an equal number of City Council members—sometimes known as councilmen or aldermen or those assholes or those fucking assholes or those fucking crooks. Members meet twice a month to bicker amongst themselves, jack up tax rates, and generally jerk around the frustrated masses.

Citywide issues and policies are the province of the mayor— historically, a pompous rich guy who siphons cash from the public till and doles out favors to his sleazebag cronies.

Elections are held annually amid the traditional ugly name-calling and cries of foul, highway robbery, and "cheater, cheater, pumpkin eater." A broadsheet daily newspaper, *The Town Whiner & Crier*, features strident editorials making everybody feel guilty for not keeping up with the onslaught of candidates and ballot measures.

Household incomes vary widely in Witt's End, though millionaires and panhandlers alike share the good ol' American feeling that they're just not making it. Nearly seventy percent of the populace reports being "one missing paycheck away from being on the street." Sixty-two percent of the people on the street say they are "one missing general-relief check away" from committing mayhem by means of a pipe bomb, an assault rifle, or a rocket-propelled grenade launcher.

During the holidays, Witt's End swells to more than twice its normal size as visitors pour in on jet flights filled with caterwauling babies or in cars filled with shedding, flea-infested dogs and screaming adolescents. Christmas is the town's major economic driver, forcing legions of cash-poor parents to within a hair's breadth of bankruptcy and/or homicidal rage. Another not-to-be-missed seasonal attraction is Tax Day, in April, when hordes of underpaid hoi polloi jam themselves into Poverty Square, hats in hand, for the ceremonial pushing of the panic button.

The average age in Witt's End is thirty-nine, though generally, inhabitants look and feel older—largely because they're lying about being thirty-nine, and because the frenetic pace of life here would make them look like a bunch of broken-down wrecks no matter what.

Computer literacy is ninety-seven percent, with one hundred percent of the online community reporting that they are bedeviled by spam, viruses, bad Wi-Fi, faulty modems, loose cable connections, hacked bill-pay accounts, keyboard glitches, and various inexplicable "ghosts in the machine."

The American Medical Association recognizes Witt's End as the nation's unofficial leader in average systolic blood pressure. A unique city monitoring program found "truly alarming spikes" during the so-called rush hour—when, ironically, the need to get there now coincides with traffic reaching a near standstill. Cardiac events peak again during the late-afternoon crunch, when, after a full day's worth of useless meetings, lollygagging, malicious email exchanges, and snafus of every ilk, there exists a need to finally, as one boss put it, "get something done, for god sakes." Stress ratchets up to a degree where many simply cannot breathe. One mid-level manager, in charge of translating Chinese-language instructions into Greek at an international modular-furniture manufacturing plant, compared the pressure to the ocean at a thousand fathoms.

Eighty percent of Witt's End residents say they are either "somewhat concerned," "moderately concerned," or "very concerned" about their health, with obsessive worry about possible health problems being the primary cause of ulcers, hives, brain aneurysms, strokes, shingles, tachycardia, prolapsed heart valves, heart-valve stenosis, and kidney failure.

Witt's End is No. 2 in the world (behind Mumbai, India) in per-capita incidence of people simply dropping dead on the sidewalk. It is believed to be the only city in America where the heads of residents spontaneously explode. The most recent case involved a mid-level manager at a commercial seafood consortium. The man was "frazzled beyond belief" trying to get fresh Atlantic oysters from point A to point B in the thick of the mother of all supply-chain quagmires. The explosion, in a hallway outside a corporate conference room, produced "a loud popping noise, like a party favor," a co-worker said.

The Witt's End Hysterical Society is collecting accounts of such events for its forthcoming commemorative book, *This Is Witt's End*.

If you are planning a trip here, be sure to visit the city's popular malware site, wwv.WittsEnd.guv/malware-deals, for a variety of newly expired coupons and restricted offers. Be sure to pack road flares and an emergency beacon.

Youngfellas:
Tales of the Fourth-Grade Mob

Lots of wise guys and horse's a-holes love to bluster about how tough it was where they came from. The beatings, the hits. Car bombs. Lifeless bodies shoved headfirst into wood chippers. Get them started, they'll go on and on, spin you stories—woe-is-me, yackety-yak—it's all jive, the same sick con job. Smack talk ringing hollow as a conga drum. They should've been raised in my old 'hood—the rotten, stinking core of suburbia. That's where you saw the real pinch of hard times, the grim face of human misery. Picket-fence hell, I call it. Grass lawns trimmed up neat as graveyards—the same bright flowers, too. Pretty as Norman Rockwell would've drawn it, except it was a cheap façade, fake as the hair on the head of that weirdo across the street.

The fact is, in my neighborhood, the rough stuff started early. Fellas got hurt. Cuts, smashed fingers. Skinned-up knees and elbows. The way I saw it, the worst instigators were the half-literate nerds, knuckleheads, and desperados of *La Nostra Quarte Grado*—the fourth-grade mob.

Latchkey delinquents. Half-pint hooligans—I heard that phrase more than once, mostly from Mr. Nelms, whose homeroom, 14B (out in the bungalows), housed a rogue's gallery of blossoming sociopaths. I can still picture the faces. Punks like Richie "Frog Legs" Franklin, who could fire a spitball all the way from the back row to the blackboard. And Carl Cowlings, a gum-chomping kingpin of contraband. "Candy Ass," we called him, because he was the main conduit from Jillian's Sweet Shop on Hempel Street right into the playground. Milk Duds. Hershey bars. Red and black licorice. Reese's. Carl could get it all. He'd stroll into Jillian's like he was Diamond Jim Brady—every morning, loading up his pockets and strutting right past the attendance office, in broad daylight, blowing bubbles of pink Bazooka gum.

In those days, Mr. Hambrick roamed the playground like a lumbering wraith, his ear-blasting steel whistle on a cord around his neck. One lousy Reese's was enough to get you busted. The mob didn't care. Vince Tolbert was another hard-core trafficker. "Vinny the Bird," we called him—a skinny little guy, but he moved a lot of Fire Sticks, Mars Bars, and M&Ms. If you wanted M&Ms, Vinny was your guy. He'd cut you a deal for only half your lunch money.

Guys like me got sucked in. You had to belong or risk the wrath of some very tough hombres. Now, don't get me wrong—I was happy to score a Hershey's or Twix from the Bird if there was nowhere else to turn. But things got out of hand. I took the drill five times that fourth-grade year. The dental drill, I'm talking about—five cavities, three on the lower. Didn't stop me, but I began to see the gang for what it was: a bunch of parasites, predators. Wouldn't surprise me a bit if they were getting kickbacks from Dr. Burke, that sadist. I think he shorted me on the Novocain just to hear me scream. The mob boys probably put him up to it.

Those jackals loved to jerk you around. They'd squish gum into the drinking fountains so the water sprayed out in a jet, blasting you up the nose. Then they'd laugh. It was all a joke to them. They even sprinkled chalk dust on Mrs. Allingham's chair just to see her tight dark skirts take on the bold white outline of her buttocks. She was the sexiest teacher we had—a sad fact in that pathetic excuse for an institution of learning. Dusted in chalk, the fair Mrs. Allingham's ample derriere stood out clear as a Warhol print of a harvest moon. Every damn time, the impudent wolves would hoot and howl all through recess.

Nothing was sacred. Speaking of recess, the dirty, grasping hands of the mob seized complete control of the recess rackets. The ringleader there was Joe Manikowski—a.k.a. "Joey M.," "Joe Skeeball," and "Joe Problemo." Chisel-nosed, wiry, a real slick-as-glass schmoozer, he was diminutive in size—only 4-foot-6—but a real muscle guy. Joey probably threatened Miss Randall—who knows? —but somehow, he wangled the position of playground ball monitor. The little creep reveled in the power. You wanted a tetherball? You had to go to Joey. Kickball? Joey. Basketball? Same deal. Every freakin' recess, Joey would stand there next to the big canvas ball bin, handing out favors the way Lucky Luciano once shelled out political bribes.

Joey ran a pay-to-play scheme. Slip him a greenback, you were in. Shoot him an ill-advised cross-eyed glance and it was game over—and we all knew it. Oh, but Joey had his favorites. Tabitha Granberry, for instance. The knock-kneed little vixen had the young Romeo wrapped around her pink nail-polished finger. That "Granberry chick," as we in Mr. Nelms's class called her—with her frizzy red hair and eyes as blue as icy Popsicles. She could flash a smile and get anything she wanted, usually a four-square ball. She'd take it and run, showing off those lean, white-as-chalk legs.

Recesses were free-for-alls. Bloodshed? Oh, yeah, I saw it myself. Ricky Mullaney got it bad one day, trying to put a hit on Ainsley Duckworth. Ricky was blocking. Everyone knew the game—touch football. The meanest racket back then. The Duck's elbow came up and landed like a crowbar on Mullaney's nose. The scene—my God, Lori Bergen nearly fainted. It looked like the restaurant lot where Gotti's henchmen gunned down Paul Castellano.

Andy Renshaw was another—he went down hard one day, right there on the playground blacktop. Fast, street-smart, a far better ball-handler than the gym rats gave him credit for. "Dandy Andy" was working his favorite hustle—hoops—when he spotted a gap in the lane and cut hard left, angling to score. The bastard was always looking for that quick score. This time, the shot was good; he was a dead-eye shooter and always one step ahead of the Fuzz. (The Fuzz being Donald "Fuzzhead" Simmons, who had hair like a Brillo pad.) We counted the deuce, but Dandy Andy crashed into the steel support pole holding up the basket. He paid the price with a cracked tooth and a lacerated lip.

The physical damage healed, but you can't just brush off the emotional scars. I'd lay a C-note on old Dandy Andy being in the nut house these days.

Conflicts flared like grease fires and were usually settled by applying a clenched fist to somebody's kisser. No one dared to call the cops—or even a teacher. I was there when brash, showboating Lyle Danziger—"Bed Bug" Danziger—ran afoul of the Haines brothers, the twins Jim and Jerry, and, in the bitter lingo of the playground, "words were exchanged." Jim got hot and made threats, and many of us feared what might happen later—that the Bug might get squashed. Sure enough, in a few weeks, Danziger was gone. I figured it was the Hoffa thing all over again. I whispered to Anna Sealey, who sat right behind me in the third row, "I bet you a Snickers bar the Bug's dead in a rock quarry. Or taking a long walk on the river bottom."

Anna looked stricken. She marched right down to the counseling office, where all those Stepford drones—Jesus, they might have been in on the hit—gave her the story that the Danzigers had moved to Tallahassee. Of all places in the world, Tallahassee? In theory, possible. But come on—were we born yesterday?

Hidden agendas, betrayals, infighting. You had to watch yourself every second. Dawdle too long getting off the bus—or getting on, for that matter—and likely as not, you'd hear about it or get poked. I know for a fact that more than a few slow movers felt the business end of a No. 2 pencil.

Thieves were thick as—well, thieves. I lost two baseball mitts, a Slinky, and a copy of *Mad* magazine, all in the same godawful month. Twice, on Fridays, when the cafeteria served my favorite— fish sticks and tater tots—I made the mistake of looking away, probably to check out some young hottie like Julie Martelle or Phoebe Greene. Looked back and my tater tots were gone. The second time, I saw right away it was Ken Willis. Caught him red-

Insults May Vary

handed; he crowed about it, actually—bragged out loud to the whole room before chucking those tots right into his big, ugly pie-hole. Wolfed them down. No ketchup either. Just ate 'em to fry my ass.

Three days later—call me crazy—I grabbed the chocolate milk off that butthead's tray and ran outside and guzzled it. A miracle I'm still alive to tell the story.

Lunch hours—good God, what a scene. Kids herded here and there like wild boar. Every day in the cafeteria line, the same faces: scowling, miserable, condemned to consuming another lousy lukewarm meal accompanied by mushy broccoli or green beans. Just like inmates queuing up for chow at San Quentin. That's probably where some of them are now.

Me? I avoided the madness of the pay-food line like it led straight to Old Sparky. Cheapskates like me, born of cheapskate parents and cheapskate grandparents—a cheapskate heritage dating back through the ages—refused to be suckered into coughing up sixty cents for a dime's worth of Salisbury steak. We had our own crew. A fair number, like Butch Reed, belonged to the lunch pail brigade. Butch lugged the same dented, cornball *Popeye* lunchbox he'd had since second grade. Pop the latch and inside it was the same blasted thing every day—a sandwich, an apple, and a mini-Thermos filled with red fruit drink. Nine times out of ten, the sandwich was baloney; I knew it, and everyone else knew it too. I would have told Butch right to his face, that's baloney—except I knew he already knew it. And we both knew damn well that I knew that he knew it. What point causing hard feelings that might escalate into a full-on incident? Still, I'd have said it, told him straight-out it was baloney—because it was baloney almost every goddamn time.

Armando DeLuna was another poor loser. Either tuna fish or egg salad on rye, day after day after day. The egg salad would be warm, and it stank to high heaven. If you sat next to him, the stench was like twin spikes up your nostrils.

I admit I was jaded. We all were. We looked down our noses at the geeky little first- and second-graders, even while we envied their spiffy metal lunch pails—*Donald Duck*, *Felix the Cat* ("what a wonderful, wonderful cat!"), *Casper the Ghost*. By fourth grade, mob pressure forced out most of the Peter Pans and Snow Whites. I clung tight as long as I could to my *Roadrunner* model with a red-capped Thermos. It vanished like a fickle capo in a summer garage sale. Killed me at the time. What could I do? Like Nicky "Banana Breath" Scobelli, I became a bag man. A lot of us did. Mike McDaniel, Tommy Dworkin, Leslie Anne Hargrove. A whole gang of us would show up at the lunch tables toting ominous brown paper sacks—and you could only guess what was inside them. A switchblade? A Luger? It might be anything.

Out would come a Baggie with a smashed-up, wet-looking Wonder Bread sandwich, glommed together with pasty-looking Underwood Deviled Ham. There'd be canned sodas, Ding Dongs, Twinkies. You had to wonder how often the feds were onto the parents for attempted murder.

As the year lurched on, I became more and more leery of those tall, shadowy figures who rolled up on Holly Street in their hatchbacks and SUVs. Slowly, as if picking up a scent in the wind, I realized the enormous, covert influence of the Five Families: the Halsteads, the Glickmans, the Mayotts, the Howertons, and the Clarks. Mob royalty, in those days. They all inhabited big-window fortresses along North Maple, Hawthorn, Cypress, and East Waverly, where the contoured lawns and leafy sycamores provided opulent cover for the goings-on within—lifestyles that can only be described as—well, I guess *idyllic* is the word.

By means of what graft, what torture, what Ponzi schemes and protection rackets did these seemingly erudite clans amass such conspicuous fortunes? Swimming pools. Billiard rooms. Libraries. Wet bars in the basement with hidden caches of *Playboy*.

Naturally, I harbored some envy of the *noblesse* bastards, the Nostra elite, and I studied them a lot more carefully than I studied U.S. geography, that's for sure. Dougie "The Firefly" Howerton's mom, Regina, was one of the puppet masters. There was no dispute about that—she conducted marionette shows in her backyard. And Jake Clark's father, stern, grizzled old Warren Clark, was a pillar of the North Maple Neighborhood Watch. He knew exactly where all the bodies were buried—mostly at Hillcrest Memorial Park, just down the street.

I was particularly intrigued by my classmate Archie "Homework" Halstead, a stork-like, fidgety kid who wore John Lennon glasses and loved whales, of all things. He claimed to have dreams—pipe dreams, I always thought—of becoming a marine biologist. Archie was a veritable electromagnet for the steely malevolence of the mob brethren. They despised him for his dorky "bowl" haircut, his gleaming blue Schwinn, and his 3.9 grade-point average.

Sure enough, late in the school year, he stopped coming to class. Rumors had it that Archie was down with the mumps, but I doubted the loose-tongued happy talk. Fearing the worst—fearing a grisly hit like the one that claimed Sonny Corleone out on the causeway—I sneaked a call to Shari Glickman, an earnest, dark-haired girl, and asked her to inquire on the QT.

Three days later, during snack break, she whispered in my ear something to the effect of, "Archie Halstead sleeps with the fishes."

The news hit me like a cattle prod—like a thousand volts surging through my fingers and toes. I later confirmed the cold reality with Fuzzhead, Dandy Andy, and a couple of other snot-nosed mobsters.

Sleeps with the fishes.

Yes—mumps-stricken Archie had used the time off from school to set up an aquarium in his bedroom.

David Ferrell

Table Talk: Of Bonbons and Bon Mots

Harken back to a glorious bygone era when conversation sparkled. When the lure of lively repartee drew patrons aplenty to amber-lit saloons and bistros. Clever witticisms were collected like pearls. A snarky rejoinder was exactly that—and sometimes more. Amid the din of voices, you could glance into the rheumy eyes of a foul-smelling coot across from you—an unshaven scarecrow in a stained gray fedora—and ponder an inscrutable mystery. Was his sly chuckle a signal of real amusement? Or disdain? Or was it that the old bird, being nearly deaf, had missed the joke but was playing along rather than admit he hadn't heard you?

What I'm talking about, now sadly lamented, was a golden age of jousting grandiloquence. To many, its yammering focal point was a particular spot in the dining room of the Algonquin Hotel in New York. The so-called Algonquin Round Table sprang up as an informal klatch of intellectuals and pseudo-intellectuals who sparred at noon luncheons while downing highballs and cheese-laden crackers. Members included a Who's Who of bon vivants drawn from the selfsame Who's Who list: the likes of George S. Kaufman, the playwright; Dorothy Parker, the droll poet and critic who was said to be capable of speaking a thousand words with a wink; and Alexander Woollcott, a vaunted journalist who, if he were alive today, surely would deny—with characteristic blunt outrage—that he devoted excessive amounts of time to carving tiny nudes out of pilfered bars of hotel soap. (To Woollcott's everlasting good fortune, he was never even accused of such a thing.)

The rhetorical pyrotechnics of the Algonquin regulars "sizzled and crackled," as one guest observed, "like flashing arcs of blue current from a Tesla coil." Reading the accounts, it's easy to take the notion one step further: those galvanizing insights, barbs, and riotous derisive hoots may have equaled, in their intensity, the sizzling and crackling of a malfunctioning electric chair. The blinding brilliance of each highly charged encounter "lit the skies and blew out the circuit breakers"—a poetic bit of metaphor you might be tempted to dismiss as nostalgic hyperbole, except it comes from one former member of the Round Table itself. These insiders never shied from brutal candor in branding themselves geniuses *nonpareil*.

Sadly, though, the Round Table dissolved after 1929; the Great Depression forced a generation of glib wiseacres to ingest humble pie and go out hawking pencils on Madison Avenue. It's well established that, for much of the ensuing century, scintillating banter fell to a low ebb. Public gathering spaces in America became somber, even morose. The drought was excruciating—millions suffered—but at last, thankfully, it is over. A worthy successor to the voluble Round Table has emerged in, of all places, Jerome, Arizona—a ramshackle ex-mining town reborn as an art colony and tourist trap on a craggy mountainside west of Sedona.

The Jerome Cabal, as I've dubbed this wondrous band of unknowns, consists of about a dozen perspicacious wits who convene Wednesdays on a coffeehouse patio overlooking the bone-dry valley.

It can be stated, unequivocally, that when the Cabal is in action—especially if Becky Mobley shows up—the air itself takes on a glow like St. Elmo's Fire, ionized by the sort of effulgence—oh God, my skin tingles to think about it. It's magic unrestrained, lightning in a bottle, theater unrivaled by any group past or present, the Round Table included. How can I possibly do it justice? Imagine: a remark here or there triggers another remark or reply, and then another, until soon enough the various thrusts and parries transform the Cabal table into a great, swashbuckling swordfight—figuratively speaking—with blood everywhere, so to say, and even severed heads scattered around, though not literally, of course.

What I mean is, things get intense. Jokes are driven home with maniacal zeal. Every zinger finds the soft tissue of the cerebral cortex. It's a hailstorm of ideas, a jangling pinball machine of noisy quips and *ratta-tat-tat-tat, bing-badda-bing-bing-bing* retorts. Surely, before long, these prodigiously talented raconteurs will gain fame beyond the parched Arizona hinterlands. But until then, it's useful to introduce a few of the core members:

Becky Mobley — Founder and kingpin. "Beck" is a retired stenographer who attributes the perpetual squint in her vibrant green eyes to the fact she is always laughing. Plus, she suffers from glaucoma. Her morbid obesity can be blamed on her ravenous appetite for bonbons, but girth has held her back not one iota. Mobley is a crossword puzzle "devoted dabbler" who shares a single-wide trailer with her three-legged Pekinese, Dolly. Even when her dermatitis is acting up, Beck can say an unfunny word like *scissors* or *garibaldi* in such a way that everyone around goes into hysterics. Her riotous inflections are especially irresistible on words ending in *ark*—like *spark, dark,* and *aardvark.*

Wilford Polk — A gangly, affable old egg farmer, Polk is a sartorial throwback in ragged flannel shirts and coveralls. (He calls them "overalls," just to gauge how others react.) He is a dead ringer for Fred Ziffel of *Green Acres* fame and admits he is often mistaken for the proverbial country bumpkin—but be forewarned: Wilford possesses a steel-grate mind and a savant's knowledge of Mohawk history, model trains, collectible matchbook covers, and poultry. Wilford likes to punctuate the remarks of other Cabal members by observing brightly, "Just like my chickens!"

Insults May Vary

Rob Clark — This remarkable, thrice-convicted sexual predator reformed himself in prison, where he survived two shiv attacks and discovered a passion for knowledge. Against daunting odds, the erstwhile pervert sprang forth from the hellish depths of incarceration as an autodidact extraordinaire. Clark boasts of being an expert on wines, cigars (he smokes up to nine a day), free will versus determinism, existentialism, statutory rape law, and futures investing. At the gift shop he operates in Jerome, he amuses patrons by quoting from countless old reruns of *Get Smart*, *Dragnet*, and *The Andy Griffith Show*. Some customers say he looks and sounds exactly like a fifty-year-old version of Barney Fife.

Millie Alexander — Alluring yet refined, loquacious yet deeply taciturn, daring and yet timid in her own way, Millie is that ethereal spirit who seems to inhabit both the *this* and the *that*, fully embodying the yin and yang of universal oneness. Smart? Oh, my GAAAAWWWWWWWD, what a head on that hunched, spindly frame! Witty? PUH-leeeeeeeaaaazzzze! This sharp-tongued housewife could certainly give Dorothy Parker a run for her money—and no doubt give Woollcott the what-for, too.

Chauncey Carmichael — A self-taught, self-aggrandizing polymath who eagerly devoted his younger self to becoming an astronaut, a satellite TV tycoon, a deep-sea explorer, and a wildcat oilman. It's rarely pointed out within the group that Chauncey failed at every last one of these endeavors, achieving none of his lofty aims—the pitiable fact being that no one would hire him for any job, anywhere. Somehow, though, he hoisted himself up from the canvas of brutally shattered dreams and discovered his true calling as a strutting dandy. His handlebar mustache, sheet-lightning grin, and inestimable charms are known from Alabama to

Zimbabwe. "Unemployed yet unshaken," he likes to say of himself. Chauncey exploits his abundant free time boning up on useless facts for a planned TV game-show appearance.

Picture these Nimitz-class eccentrics—and six or seven more, equally gifted at verbal jiu-jitsu—engaged in a free-for-all on some intriguing topic of the day, such as gasoline prices or personal grooming. That is the essence of the Jerome Cabal. In the three years I've been showing up at meetings, I've come to expect—well, of course, I expect the expected, because expectations are part and parcel of what I expect in life—but all the while I half-expect the unexpected, too. It's so hard to predict. Most of the time, I really don't know what will happen.

Here's a moment: Millie glancing up to see Rob Clark arrive, his signature slick-as-Pennzoil mullet replaced by an austere new buzz cut.

"Rob, you finally got a haircut!" Millie exclaimed.

"Hell," he said, sneering, "I got 'em all cut."

You can't make this stuff up. Nothing is off-limits—no topic too obscure, too high-falutin', or lowbrow for the twitching minds of these eclectic thinkers. One minute they're speculating about the nature of ice volcanoes on Pluto; the next, they're debating whether Harry Houdini could have escaped from a diving bell in the Challenger Deep.

More than a few rollicking discussions are inspired by the simple tableau of tourists strolling down the street out front.

"Look at the tuchus on that one!" Wilford Polk observed one day, his voice rising like a teakettle on the boil. "How does that human hippopotamus ever fit in a theater seat?"

"Maybe he streams movies at home instead of paying big bucks to sit in a theater," Rob said. "Ever think of that, Poindexter?"

"Whoa, Wilford's right—that is one substantial derriere!" Chauncey declared.

"Who are you to talk about appearances?" Beck challenged, eyeing Chauncey's mustache. "You've got a freakin' caterpillar on your lip! Another week and it'll be a cocoon."

A cocoon! How she delivered that one, in a fresh instant, is an oratorical miracle. Humor flows in a ceaseless torrent, like hail during a downpour or sludge from a broken sewer line. If one Cabal member doesn't come up with a crack, you can bet another one will.

Truly, I can count on one hand—or maybe two—the number of awkward silences when they all sat and tried to think of something clever to say but couldn't. Typically, free association reigns; meetings might be likened to a tumultuous group session in a psychiatric facility—but in a good way. Beck has a fondness for going after Chauncey, accusing him of all manner of picayune transgressions, from grammatical lapses to smelling like a donkey on hot days.

"You really mangled that verb agreement," she might say, causing Chauncey's head to jerk up, his dark eyes flashing fiery indignation.

"I did not!"

"You did."

"Did not."

"Did."

"Did not."

"Did."

"Did not."

They'll go back and forth fifteen, twenty times, while the others grin and guffaw and make derisive snorting noises.

As in New York, when the original Round Table was in its heyday, local gossip provides grist for much of the discussion. A recent subject was Miles Frantz, the head bartender at the Jerome Saloon. Frantz was rumored to be seeing a widow in town while also dating a waifish former nurse just down the highway in Sedona. Carmichael observed that it was hard to imagine even one woman interested in a man such as Frantz, never mind two.

With the Cabal as tribunal, the hapless bartender was put on trial in absentia and essentially convicted of being a dolt, a heel, and a sorry-looking cuss who should shave his billy-goat beard and trim his fingernails once in a while.

When the subject of yoga came up, Beck didn't know what it was; however, the focus swiftly shifted from Tibetan yogis to Yogi Bear and then to Yosemite Sam and Bugs Bunny. Wilford's throaty imitation of Bugs's famous refrain, "What's up, doc?" caused Millie to grouse about her latest doctor visit:

"What was up?" she moaned. "My blood sugar. My goddamn type 2 diabetes." It was already causing numbness in her toes.

Plus, she said, "I rolled out of the sack yesterday and thought I'd stepped on a carpet tack. Come to realize it was only diabetic nerve pain."

"I did step on a carpet tack," Beck intoned. "Just last January. Put me in the ER."

Historians have pointed out that the Algonquin Round Table was far greater in *toto* than the mere sum of its parts. The same surely is true of the Cabal. I've filled seventeen steno books so far documenting their magic. My long-range hope is to compile a book—possibly a full archive—to memorialize the best of the best of the classic moments. Like when Millie pointed out that the Sedona High School cheerleaders had finished last in a team competition in Phoenix.

"Poor girls sure laid an egg," said Rob.

"Just like my chickens," Wilford added.

Oh my God! One time Beck described a mishap in her kitchen: In trying to re-ignite a pilot light, she touched off an explosion and fireball that singed off her eyebrows.

"It was the first hot flash I'd felt in twenty minutes," she cracked.

Oh, Jee-SUS Christ Lord God Almighty!

There was such uproarious laughter I can't even describe it. You'd have thought she'd just sat on a whoopee cushion.

ART REVIEW:
A Hard Look at 'Lady Godiva's Belly Button'

Let me preface my critique of the artist Schadrach's latest abstract-expressionist painting, *Lady Godiva's Belly Button*, by acknowledging that a century from now—or perhaps two centuries at most—this drippy, modest-sized (14 by 18 inches) acrylic-on-balsawood inspiration, so clearly influenced by Pollock, Diebenkorn and, dare I say, Raphael, will fetch $800 million easy at some hoity-toity auction house where suckers drive up in Brinks trucks. Schadrach has an undeniable gift for creating interesting puddles of pigment in varying colors, and, for whatever inscrutable reasons, the art establishment (i.e., the Art Establishment) has embraced this gap-toothed, Polish-born émigré with the zeal of a six-year-old embracing a Yorkshire terrier.

At least four of Schadrach's earlier works—including the moody, indigo-laden homage to El Greco, *Holy Toledo, Ohio*, which graced the November cover of *Modern Museum*—already stand alongside the most hallowed art pieces of modern culture. Bill Gates is said to have paid $72 million for Schadrach's green-flecked *Grassy Field*, and an anonymous collector, believed by many to be bitcoin tycoon Vladimir Triske, shelled out $89 million for the somewhat darker companion work, *Weedy Patch With Oil Can*.

Curators at the Guggenheim were ecstatic last spring when they were able to acquire (reportedly for $216 million) Schadrach's most controversial piece: the circular, all-black oil-on-canvas painting initially known as *Untitled Spherical Object*, later re-dubbed *Circle Sans Title*, which had garnered so much attention at the Louvre. The point of the Guggenheim's purchase—and of the painting itself, for that matter—escapes this reviewer, but certainly the work marked the beginning of Schadrach's much-ballyhooed thematic pursuit of roundness, a dominant element of the artist's *oeuvre* for the past decade.

This takes us now, metaphorically speaking, directly into Ms. Godiva's navel—a place that, through the lens of Schadrach's singularly skewed vision, becomes both engrossing and somehow disorienting—filled with lint, as it were. A bit of backstory is relevant here, inasmuch as Schadrach (real name Linus Jankowski) has previously, with discernible diligence, avoided rendering the human form, either in whole or in part. As he explained to one German television station, "People don't interest me—and they're hard to paint." This attitude was most evident when Schadrach famously refused a generous commission to paint a pastel portrait of Saudi Arabian princess Lydia Ghatami, even after she offered to be depicted only as a cube-like silhouette. "Just say it's me," she implored the artist, according to *Dannehoken* magazine. The affronted princess has since sued the New York-based Schadrach in U.S. District Court, alleging intentional infliction of emotional distress.

The story of Godiva, however, appears to have inspired Schadrach to deviate from past patterns. (I use the term "deviate" advisedly; Schadrach is, after all, a registered sex offender.) The art historian Clement L. Clement notes that Schadrach's paternal great-great-great-great grandfather, Lionel, had a cousin who knew a woman in Normandy, France, with connections to the town of Coventry, England, where the Lady Godiva legend was born. These mysterious "connections" may or may not have included the fabled Peeping Tom who accosted the fair noblewoman near the end of her audacious ride. It is widely speculated—albeit unproven—that Schadrach himself is a direct descendant of the despicable pervert.

Insults May Vary

Whatever the case, young Linus grew up entranced with the Godiva legend. The idea of a nude maiden galloping through town on horseback, her golden hair streaming in the wind, reoccurs throughout many of his early diaries and unpublished memoirs. His own unrepressed longing was to be borne about the village (any village, Clement says) on a magnificent steed, and later to "commit wild carnal aggression" (his words) on a "suitably alluring young vixen." That a court-appointed psychiatrist classified him as "dangerous and quite possibly insane" in a 2019 legal filing seems only to have enhanced Schadrach's considerable mystique—and thus given unintended impetus to his skyrocketing career.

A key creative question in assessing *Lady Godiva's Belly Button* is as obvious as the horn on a rhinoceros: Why only her belly button? The woman herself was reputed to be radiant, and the drama of her famous ride begs for artistic interpretation, particularly in the abstract-expressionist realm. Many experts agree that the only worthy analog is Marcel Duchamp's *Nude Descending a Staircase, No. 2*—an acknowledged masterpiece that ignored anatomical realism in favor of seductive geometries and a boldly lascivious title. Schadrach's unholy obsession with Duchamp led to his own failed cubist piece, a rip-off provocatively entitled *Nude Cartwheeling Down the Stairs, No. 28*—a mess of converging lines and planes that was said to show, in inscrutable *Where's Waldo?* fashion, a carelessly discarded banana peel alongside the discombobulated figure. It is my opinion that the banana peel is, in fact, discernible under a frenzy of dark, squiggly lines, though I disagree that this tasteless touch wrecks the piece. A more obvious fact is that the work's basic composition and overall execution are simply horrendous.

No matter. Quality and taste appear to mean nothing to the small, bone-headed circle of so-called "intellectuals" to whom Schadrach is the next messiah. Among these deluded sycophants is author and art critic Bernard C. Westhaven, who excuses Schadrach for refusing to retell, visually, a story as familiar as Godiva's. Like other cretins of his ilk, Westhaven actually commends Schadrach for gravitating to the one physical feature that perfectly symbolizes the subject's unclad state without creating on the canvas a meme of exploitation or—God forbid—pornography.

Point taken. But my difficulties with Schadrach's painting have less to do with his decision to concentrate exclusively on the navel than with his depiction of that navel—specifically, the fact that he's given it such a jarring, flamboyantly colored, almost kaleidoscopic treatment. Timothy Leary would not have viewed a woman's belly button through such a dissonant prism, with shards of brilliant yellow, red, blue, and green clashing in a gravelly stew of competing hues—all within the great dark bowl of the navel itself.

In terms of balance, the painting is problematic—though perhaps to some advantage. Tension is clearly evident. Note, for example, what appears to be a long vermillion "pin" or "needle" piercing the navel in the upper-right quadrant. This effect is surely intentional on Schadrach's part, for he (or someone) has written "Ouch!" in microscopic letters at the juncture of this "object" and the navel itself.

Should we allow for the possibility that sabotage was committed by a vandal with a proclivity for producing infinitesimal graffiti—and that Schadrach failed to notice? This reviewer thinks not. More likely, the blatant subtlety (to coin a phrase, for the word can be read only through a magnifying glass) is yet further evidence that Schadrach's mental deterioration—let's call it what it is—continues unabated. *Ouch?* Sad to say, it is the art aficionado who ultimately suffers the sting of this dubious creative touch—or should I be more blunt and brand it an abomination?

Whatever force exists in the painting—and some viewers do sense power—derives largely from geometrical shapes: triangles and diamonds of bold pigment afloat like scissor-cut confetti on a blanket of somber tones. Here again, fans applaud the artist's bold vision, while I rue the reckless sausage-making involved in throwing together colors, willy-nilly. Consider, for a moment, the filigree of blinding pink convex lines forming a thin visible net over the work as a whole. The only clear interpretation of this effect is

Insults May Vary

that Schadrach has elected to depict Godiva's navel as an "outie" and not an "innie"—which naturally invites speculation about midwife practices in pre-Columbian Europe. We are left to imagine, perhaps forever, how much more effective the rendering might have been (and alluring, too) if this overly celebrated dimwit (Schadrach) had only given us a lattice of concave lines instead.

In a veritable snake pit of writhing, contrasting brushstrokes in the lower left part of the painting, there's one deep crimson line that caught my attention—thin, about an inch long, and angled upward from left to right. I really think it should have been orange.

Also, there seems an overly generous amount of vermillion in this work—why? Additional flecks of fuchsia, and perhaps even some little dots of blue and/or green, might have created a more interesting effect. He's got some red and yellow dots in there—what's wrong with blue?

The French press reports that Schadrach, having spent sixteen months on the painting, is on an extended tour of Africa and Asia, relaxing prior to his next project. *Le Monde* seems to have it on good—albeit anonymous—authority that Schadrach intends to devote much of the next year and beyond to a definitive interpretation of the late Princess Diana's nose.

Given the sensitivities involved, and the wild potential for extrapolation, this critic can only hope that the pigment-dripping virtuoso can get his head screwed on right before his trip is over and he assaults the canvas again.

David Ferrell

The Lowdown On Famous Secret Societies

As Mark Twain once said—or very possibly thought to himself without actually expressing it out loud—it is easier to ice skate up a mountain road in a tornado than it is to probe the inner machinations of the great secret societies.

The vast majority of secret societies are simply not well publicized. You almost never see them touting their sinister rites on the web or on highway billboards. No news is good news, as far as these strange birds are concerned.

Still, paradoxically, certain covert organizations have made quite a name for themselves over the years—sometimes for the very lengths they'll go to avoid attracting attention. An obvious case in point is Skull and Bones, a furtive band of elitist yahoos that has existed at Yale University for nearly two centuries. The club's surreptitious nature is so deeply ingrained that some former members purposely develop dementia—or become hermits living off the grid—rather than risk inadvertently revealing the organization's secret handshakes, rituals, and buzzwords.

What does Skull and Bones do?

Why does it even exist?

Wouldn't you like to know!

Only this much is certain: The name derives from key components of the human body. The fundamental purpose of Skull and Bones seems to be to keep the activities of Skull and Bones a carefully guarded secret. As to the specific nature of those activities, there has emerged, over the years, a smattering of innuendo and supposition: that "Bonesmen" drink Scotch, chase women, chit-chat amongst themselves (sometimes while indulging in a whiff of the reefer), and convene in the dark of night to practice pagan (or non-pagan) rituals in a funky old meeting hall known affectionately (or sarcastically) as *The Tomb*.

Scuttlebutt holds that, back when collecting severed heads was all the rage, initiates managed to purloin the noggin of the dead Mexican revolutionary, Pancho Villa. It's a disturbing possibility that the artifact may still lie somewhere in the club's basement—a gruesome target of gnawing rats. The broader point is this: Skull and Bones represents just one organization in a wide array of secret societies that are out there doing God-knows-what any flippin' time they want to.

The Rosicrucians.

The Freemasons.

The Hermetic Order of the Golden Dawn.

I'd even include the Mickey Mouse Club in this dubious roll call.

Chances are your next-door neighbor slips off every Wednesday night to some faceless conclave where members wear pointy noses, inhale helium, and talk like that nitwit on Fox News.

Consider the following short list of the most notoriously secretive of the secret societies. These groups wield enormous power—or, in a few cases, no power at all—while remaining so deep in the weeds that even America's top intelligence agencies regard them as non-entities. It's a miracle that I've managed to scrape up the following information, presented here as a public service.

The Cleveland Clandestine Club

No one has ever been able to determine who these Bozos are, what they do, or where they meet. This deplorable fact is true even though the club is thought to be Ohio's oldest benevolent—or possibly malevolent—organization, predating the Buckeye Brigade and the Ohio Ghosts of the Revolution.

Adherents of the CCC may number well over one thousand—unless they number fewer than one thousand. Or fewer than one hundred, even. Today's highest-ranking members have been rigorously indoctrinated in the time-honored ways of the cult; that's a prevailing theory that has yet to be disproven. Surely very sophisticated brainwashing techniques are practiced, involving a lot of glad-handing and smug self-congratulation. Secret bylaws, rites, and traditions might well be handed down from one generation to the next, perhaps dating back as far as America's founding fathers—who knows?

Such tantalizing morsels have spawned many attempts by outsiders to investigate—mostly in vain. The nonprofit *Ohio Gotcha Council* recently boasted a rare coup by discovering a CCC manifesto posted on the dark web. Carrying the byline Joseph Ichabod Blow (a likely pseudonym), the diatribe consisted mainly of "nonsense text"—a deliberately incomprehensible hodgepodge of ciphers and cuneiforms. Thus far only a small section of it, a limerick, has been decoded:

Friends, trust your gut-level hunch,
We're a very mysterious bunch.
We can't even say,
If we're home or away,
We're prolly at the bar drinking lunch.

The West L.A. Anti-Social Society

Upon its creation in a Culver City garage in 1926, this "iconic iconoclastic organization" was so secretive that not a single person joined it—or even knew about it—for perhaps a quarter of a century. This despite a wave of anti-social fervor then sweeping Los Angeles. (And which, truth be told, has never abated.)

Insults May Vary

Founder Les McKunkle, a man who "hated everyone and everything," railed against the endless parties, dinners, salons, powwows, booze fests, round tables, and otherwise unstrained hobnobbing so common in the city he loathed. On top of that, he hated the press. Wishing his subversive clan to be "utterly exclusive, as well as reclusive," he barred even his own wife, Rosamund, from joining—a decision that proved disastrous for him. Sued for divorce, McKunkle lost his home, half his fortune, and two upper incisors, blasted out by some kind of steel rod or tire iron wielded by a thug Rosamund was accused of hiring. (She and the attacker were acquitted by a criminal jury.)

The Anti-Social Society more or less languished until the late 1950s, when McKunkle's articles of incorporation were put to use, in Hancock Park, to line the cage of a cockatiel named Wally Bird. A servant boy saw and embraced the rambling screed and soon grew the organization to more than 3,000 members—all sworn to despise their fellow man and make Los Angeles an inhospitable hellhole.

The group's activities today are believed to concentrate on provoking traffic accidents during the evening rush hour. Some members are also suspected of cranking up disco and hip-hop music in densely populated neighborhoods after midnight.

Shari Philpott's Leper Colony and Infectious Ebola Disease Halfway House

The name and accompanying warning signs are emblazoned in red above the barricaded, windowless doors of this society's warehouse headquarters in a gritty Baltimore industrial zone. Who gains entry here? It's hard to know; getting inside may be more difficult than breaching strategic nerve centers of the Pentagon.

One certainty: Lepers and Ebola patients are kept at bay at all costs. Not even a plumber is admitted without undergoing a seven-day quarantine. The lie that the building is a level-five infectious disease facility is meant, of course, to discourage visitors—a tactic that works like mustard gas. The massive entry doors swing open only at midnight, when members drift stealthily toward the fortress-like structure from out of the night's blackness, slipping noiselessly inside. Some, thought to be "exalted" leaders, show up wearing the same sort of ominous dark hoods sported by the Zodiac killer; lesser members and newer recruits simply cover their heads and faces with paper bags.

So fearful are they of being identified that most refuse to cut eyeholes in the bags. Sadly, at least six members of the society have been killed in recent years by wandering into traffic.

Eponymous founder Shari Philpott is regarded within the Baltimore underground as a fictional personality based on a transgender reinterpretation of Howard Hughes. Her real name remains unknown.

The Covert Anonymous Hush-Hush League

Self-proclaimed Grand Poobah Roland Crowder forced this once-thriving, world-famous social club to completely reinvent itself in 2011. Besides adopting a new name, the organization purged 4,000 "life members" from its rolls and shifted its bimonthly meetings to a spartan hideaway situated off the grid in northern Utah.

After "going dark," the newly clandestine society "imploded with a force of one thousand megatons," in the bitter assessment of one ex-insider—a man who had spent $60,000 for a "Premium Platinum Membership" and lost it all. In a tumultuous span of only eight weeks, membership in the Hush-Hush League shrank to a measly forty-six hardcore zealots. Jilted ex-clubbers had no clue where, when, or even if meetings were still being held. Ultimately, they took the extraordinary step of hiring a private detective to ascertain why their beloved organization—which once drew tens of thousands to its open-air festivals and public sing-alongs

Insults May Vary

throughout the West—had vanished virtually overnight.

Legal woes were revealed to be a strong factor. Crowder was under enormous pressure to stop promoting the society under its original name: The Mormon Tabernacle Choir.

During the acrimonious two years in which the underground organization reconstituted itself, a disgruntled faction—led by renegade outdoorsman Richard Milsap—broke away to create their own rival secret organization: The Royal Canadian Mounted Police. That defection (derided by some as "The Defecation") left the reeling Hush-Hush League limping along with just twelve adherents—or technically thirteen, since Paul Lopat was allowed to register his split personalities, Paul and Paulette, as separate individuals.

In 2020, Crowder moved the society's official headquarters from Provo to a weather-beaten grass hut on a beach in Puerto Rico. Most followers, like Crowder himself, were by then on the lam from federal indictments. But what a cast of characters it was: A woman named Irina could play the harp with her toes. The society, slightly larger now, is believed to remain active, holding monthly meetings at a compound of abandoned chicken coops in San Juan.

Peeping Toms of America

Touting itself as the nation's only elite secret club devoted to voyeurism, the Peeping Toms—or "Peepers"—have achieved meteoric growth since shedding their early moniker, The Royal Canadian Mounted Police.

The group's motto, *"Wow, Look at That!"*, has galvanized an avid core group of ex-CIA spies, mall cops, compulsive snoops, busybodies, creeps, sleazeballs, registered sex offenders, and perverts of virtually every ilk. Self-styled potentate Richard Milsap, a.k.a. "Deviant Dick," spends weeks planning elaborate "cheesecake runs," in which devotees travel by bus or car caravan to a pre-selected window—usually a bedroom or bathroom window—where they zero in on the chosen target, invariably a female considered to be (in the society's catchy vernacular) "a sexy babe," "smokin' hot," or "one really freakin' hot mama."

Monthly meetings, now held in Boise, Idaho, generally devolve into a yuk-fest as the drunken reprobates relive their despicable late-night forays by gawking at photographs and videos.

Inasmuch as every suspected participant in this reprehensible debauchery is wanted in at least nine states, the Peepers have become more secretive than ever. A planned year-end banquet was recently canceled.

The Brotherhood of the Pinkie Ring

John Henry Magoo, a.k.a. "Old Man Magoo," had a brainstorm when he drafted plans to create his own top-secret clique in 2015. Members would be able to identify each other instantly, anywhere in the world, by means of a distinctive gold pinkie ring—a gleaming band inlaid with black onyx forming a five-pointed star.

Clever though it was, the scheme had an obvious flaw: the ring was a dead giveaway to some sort of tacit affiliation. Magoo therefore decreed that members would buy and own the ring (the latest discounted "club price" was $1,899), but no one would actually wear it. Instead, initiates signal each other by holding aloft a single bare pinkie finger and hissing, "Shhhhhhhh!"

The "Pinkie Brethren," as acolytes are known—and Magoo in particular—stand as ultimate examples of the shadowy realm of opaque liaisons. No one has any idea of the total membership. Followers are considered to be a misfit band of frauds, wraiths, and doppelgängers.

Take "Old Man" Magoo: He is only twenty-seven and barely looks eighteen. His given name is not John Henry; he stole that from the steel-driving folk hero. He is not even a Magoo—a name he ripped off from a cartoon character.

Strip away the false identity, and Magoo turns out to be Larry

Insults May Vary

Sears, a laid-off Detroit auto worker who is not even, as it turns out, Larry Sears. He stole the name from the department store chain. Unmask that fraudulent persona and—Jesus Christ—he's Baron Carl Hilton Doubletree, a Kansas City hotel clerk. Ah, but crack the surface of that poorly conceived façade, and you find out he's actually Matt Damon Diesel, who sheepishly admits that he operates a small bed and breakfast in Rancho Mirage, California—which isn't quite true. In fact, he tends sheep on a ranch in Bozeman, Montana, where the locals know him as Vin Diesel McConaughey, a transsexual who previously went by the name Hillary Rodham Beyoncé, a.k.a. Hillary Swank Sorvino, a.k.a. Meryl Swank-Streep Streisand—although earlier records, when she was a minor, are now sealed.

David Ferrell

A Memory to Savor: The Great Food Fight at Spago

What are we to believe when semi-reliable sources say no, a certain thing never happened, and yet the rumors and innuendos persist? My own inclination is to wonder: What are they hiding? Why such emphatic denials?

I've devoted years now to patching together a cohesive narrative in the face of dogged recalcitrance—even threats. The incident itself might seem trivial: a food fight at one of Beverly Hills' most famous eateries. Yet the pandemonium involved, and the A-list nature of the combatants, turned that long-ago, otherwise forgettable Friday night at Spago into an event for the ages.

Never mind that not a single witness has ever agreed to go on the record. The following chronicle—necessarily drawn from anonymous second-, third-, and even fourth-hand accounts—serves up a frightening glimpse into what might well have occurred during an alleged incident of pure gastronomical madness.

It was just past 8:30 p.m., a peak hour on a peak night, when George Clooney and his entourage—a party of eight—moved haphazardly from the bar into one of the main dining areas, trailing the maître d'. Sartorially resplendent, as always, Clooney wore a white cashmere jacket and matching velour riding pants. He caught sight of Quentin Tarantino, seated near the far wall, and made a playful gesture with his index finger, as if firing at him with a pistol.

Clooney's broad grin indicated a fine mood—and why not? The popular matinee idol had just won an International Press award and had signed to star in a new spy caper that would bring him yet another obscene windfall of cash. He hadn't yet noticed that, far to his left, Jay Leno was dining with a party of nine headed by a corporate honcho from NBC.

Aware that Clooney hadn't seen him, Leno, on impulse—as a favorite prank—reached out via special-delivery airmail: that is, he lifted a soft-shell crab from a viscous pool of chili aioli (a full platter lay in front of him) and sailed the pricey crustacean, Frisbee-style, toward the back of Clooney's head. The whirling sea creature traveled along a flawless longitude but an inadequate latitude: it fell short of Clooney's head and instead struck the actor's shoulder, depositing on the brilliant white arm of Clooney's jacket a gooey brownish stain roughly the size and shape of a tarantula.

Startled—no, *shocked* is the better word—Clooney regarded the defilement of his $2,000 coat. He could not have looked more horrified had he discovered an actual, live, hairy-legged tarantula crawling its way toward his ear. Pawing frantically at the impact spot, Clooney somehow caught sight of, in the general vicinity of Leno, another celebrity patron: Brad Pitt, who had watched the crab in full flight. Pitt was laughing hysterically. Clooney's instant conclusion was that Pitt had flung the unwelcome food bomb.

At that point, a pressure gasket surely must have given way inside Clooney's brain. According to my main source—an ex-employee of Spago who has never been convicted of any felony, never mind perjury—Clooney glared at his pal and mouthed the words: *"You die, sucker!"*

Exercising remarkable agility, Clooney bounded forward and seized the only retaliatory weapon at hand: a meatball in wine sauce perched atop a mound of tagliatelle pasta. It is neither here nor there that the meatball was not Clooney's—it belonged to another regular patron of Spago, Lenore "Tippie" Roth, a local hair stylist. Had it been Scarlett Johansson's meatball, or Emily Blunt's, or even Steven Spielberg's, the result surely would have been the same. Clooney grabbed the meatball with no apparent regard as to its rightful owner and, single-mindedly, pivoted and hurled the densely baked planetoid at Pitt with a velocity that might have earned him—I exaggerate only slightly—a signing bonus to join the pitching staff of the Dodgers.

Regrettably, Clooney's control was no better than that of certain relievers who were considered responsible for L.A.'s precipitous drop in the baseball standings. Fingers slick with wine sauce, Clooney allowed the meatball to sail well wide of Pitt's table. It might have hit no one, or some anonymous yahoo, but on this star-studded night—so soon after the press awards—the tomato-y orb happened to land like a musket ball on the cheekbone of Javier Bardem, exploding on impact.

The mercurial Bardem was not the type to take a meatball in the eye—or just below the eye—without returning fire. He had been enjoying one of the many off-menu specialty entrées and desserts prepared for the occasion by Wolfgang himself. No one can be sure exactly what Bardem scooped in his bare hand and dispatched Clooney's way. At least two third-hand witnesses swear that the glowering Bardem had been halfway through a brandy-soaked banana-split flambé.

"Whatever it was," one cousin of a fourth-hand eyewitness said, "it sure made a mess."

Shrieks pierced the air as a melty conglomeration of ice cream, syrup, and whipped topping splattered the camera-ready faces and bespoke haute couture of the glitterati. Don Cheadle and Julia Roberts were among those soiled by the salvo. *#TheBardemFreakOut*, as half a million Twitter (later "X") users hashtagged it, was the "torch that put the fire to the nitroglycerin," in the words of celebrity blogger Alden Horowitz.

In the next few frenetic moments, at least nine guests rose in unison to launch attacks on Bardem. A lesser number—six or seven—began an assault on Clooney, their perceived scapegoat for the melee. Seen flying in various directions were great globs of risotto with chanterelle mushrooms, salmon pizza with goat cheese, black sea bass with sweet corn succotash, and oysters dripping with red wine and horseradish sauce—just for starters.

The noise became cacophonous.

"*Banzai!*" shouted Tarantino as he flung a heaping handful of pasta—many later surmised it was pesto farfalle with summer squash—in the general direction of Morgan Freeman. Whether or not Freeman was an intentional target remains unclear; in any event, the payload only partially struck the top of Freeman's head and did most of its damage at the table behind him, landing on the chin and neck of a young blonde rumored to have been an extra in *Killing Eve*.

Freeman, incensed, snatched a pan-roasted Jidori chicken breast from a passing tray and sent the bird flying on a low migratory path toward a table across the room. A dozen or so well-heeled revelers there were celebrating a woman's 95th birthday. The man most directly hit—a silver-haired dandy who was visibly tanked on vodka martinis—reacted as if the frontal lobe of his brain had been fricasseed with a welding torch. The apoplectic septuagenarian sacrificed his entire entrée of vegetable lasagna by slinging it, plate and all, discus-style, into a crowd at the bar.

Bedlam begat bedlam. A waiter named Cary, or Gary, or possibly Harry or Larry—conspicuous for his kinky red hair—was seen darting into the kitchen and returning with four cartons of raw eggs. Sharing the oblong projectiles with random customers nearby, the soon-to-be-terminated assailant opened fire on both the bar crowd and the sitting ducks occupying tables along the front wall of the courtyard. Cary (or Gary, whoever he was) proved to possess better aim than Clooney. In his final actions as a Spago employee, he nailed five or six unsuspecting individuals in the head or face, breaking one old-timer's nose. (The red-haired human bazooka has since been spotted sweeping floors at the Burger King on Sepulveda Boulevard.)

At some point, while shattered shells and egg yolks were dripping over the likes of Cheadle, Kristen Bell, and Tina Fey, mere bedlam exploded into a level of chaos resembling Omaha Beach. Enterprising patrons stormed the kitchen to fetch their own eggs, bananas, tomatoes, meatballs, and pots and platters of spaghetti and ravioli. Tables were toppled to form shields against the onslaught.

Julianne Moore, who later said she was "minding my own business . . . just trying to have a nice dinner," wound up with both nostrils stuffed with tiramisu. Susan Sarandon hurled a sesame-seared cream cheese dumpling that hit Michael Keaton in the ear. Keaton appeared unaware of who threw the dumpling—nor did he seem to care. Moving spasmodically, like a short-circuiting animatronic figure, he rose to his feet, looked wildly about, and put his full body weight behind a hefty slice of lava cake that landed flush on the forehead of an attorney from Martin, Wescott & Rosenfeld. At least some of the fragmenting dessert ended up in Leno's hair.

Meanwhile, Clooney had not yet wearied of the fight—far from it. He continued to play hardball with compressed spheres of ground beef. By one count, he managed to fire "ten or eleven" meatballs, stolen from adjoining tables, hitting Brad Pitt twice. One missile either bloodied his lip or splattered Pitt's face with marinara sauce. Or both.

An executive from Universal Pictures took a Cadillac margarita square in the beak—fortunately, only the tequila and mixer in a slushy floe of blended ice. The glass itself shattered on the bar's gleaming antique cash register. Facts became difficult to sort out; not even combatants could keep track of who was attacking whom, and to what effect. One report held that Salma Hayek was conked on the noggin by a champagne bottle. The claim was later "corrected" to indicate that it was Hayek who raised the bottle and bopped the head of another patron—identity unknown—in supposed retaliation for having an asparagus spear jammed in her ear.

"No one could stop—literally no one could stop," one blogger wrote. "It was literally the wildest thing that's ever happened on planet Earth."

True or not, it exceeded the minimum technical standards of a donnybrook.

Insults May Vary

Pizza slices flying. Calamari. Blueberry cheesecake. Sautéed halibut with zucchini purée.

Screams. Threats.

Ruined shoes. Deep, ground-in stains.

A third- or fourth-hand witness, with connections to the Gersh Agency, reported that toward the end of the fracas, horrified patrons observed a man lying face-down, spread-eagle, a dozen feet from the bar, his hair looking like seaweed—wet and matted with whiskey, egg yolk, and chocolate fudge. He appeared to be in distress, making gasping, throaty noises.

The sounds, as later recreated by a purported witness, were something like:

"Huuh-ga, huuh-ga, huuh, huuuh, huuUGH, ha-gaaa—"

Three good Samaritans—one with a black eye and crème brûlée slathered across her cheek—disengaged from the madness long enough to dial the paramedics.

Fortunately, the man was OK. He turned out to be Tim Burton. The famous director wasn't hurt or sick—he was simply laughing his fool head off.

David Ferrell

A Special Wise Guy: The Advice Guru

Dear Advice Guru,

For the past several years, I've become increasingly obsessed with the idea of having sex with an animal—maybe a sheep, which is my main fantasy, or a llama, or even an orangutan. This fall, my sister is getting married. She would like me to give her a particular style of Tiffany standing lamp as a wedding gift. Is it all right if I give her an air-fryer instead?

—Tormented in Tallahassee

Dear Tormented,

If your sister's marriage is a typical modern union, it will end soon enough in a rancorous divorce. Let's hope the flaring passions don't explode into a grisly murder that ends up on one of those true-crime TV shows.

Given the woeful possibilities, I wouldn't invest too much in a gift. Tiffany lamps can cost a bundle—and even a quality air-fryer is pricey. What about an electric can opener instead? They're sturdy and extremely useful for a newlywed hoping to enjoy a repast of alphabet soup, chili con carne, corned beef hash, or literally dozens of other gut-packing delights.

Better yet, skip the can opener (even those can be expensive) and simply wrap a few cans of tuna fish or sardines in festive paper with a bright bow. Both are rich in heart-healthy omega-3s. A "fancy" bottle of ketchup probably wouldn't go to waste either. Now that's a gift from the heart.

Dear Advice Guru,

My 22-year-old nephew lost his job and moved in with my husband and me. At first things were okay, but after a month or two, we began noticing changes in his behavior. He screams and pounds on our bedroom door during the night as a sort of running joke. He steals from my purse and George's wallet to buy vodka and cocaine and throws noisy parties at our house without permission. Several times I've come home to find 20 or 30 people in the pool, many of them drunk, the women usually topless, and music blasting so loud it could literally shatter your eardrums. He also insults my hair, my figure, and my nose. Are we wrong to ask him to move out?

—**Going Insane in Key Biscayne**

Dear Going Insane,

Sadly, you seem to be weighing your own somewhat selfish interests against the needs of your young, fun-loving, and probably quite vulnerable nephew.

You say this impressionable lad—only 22!—lost his job. How traumatic for him! Have you done anything to support this poor soul beyond letting him crash at your place? Truly caring individuals would sacrifice a little sleep, a little cash, and a little peace and quiet now and then.

But you? You write to me whining about how your eardrums are "literally" shattering from party music? Literally?

Hear me now, my delicate flower: This whole me-me-me attitude is appalling. My God, have you even *considered* what might happen if you kick this spirited but down-on-his-luck boy to the curb?

Picture him in the squalor of a homeless encampment—your own flesh and blood—lying like a dead catfish on the grimy sidewalk, clothes soaked in vomit, and a howling hurricane tearing at his only shelter: a crumbling cardboard box. Picture lightning striking. Picture balcony plants crashing down. He could die from exposure. From a drug overdose. From bird flu. He could be run over. Or gunned down by a meth-addled wacko with an assault rifle—all because *you* couldn't tolerate his joyful partying.

Did you think of that, huh? Shame on you. Don't write to me again.

Dear Advice Guru,

My wife Pamela and I have been married for eight years. Her behavior lately has been puzzling. When we first met—at a cocktail mixer for divorced singles—she was as sweet as can be. I can't even describe how sweet—just the sweetest little sweetcakes you can imagine. But now in her forties, I see a lot of pent-up hostility. One night I woke up with a huge welt on my head and our bedside lamp shattered on the floor. Another time she grabbed my nose with a pair of pliers and twisted it with all her might. Last month I caught her attaching something to the underside of my car, which turned out to be a bomb.

Is it possible she's going through "the change"? Could it be genetic, or some unresolved psychological issue from childhood? Also, might she still be angry that I slept with her daughter for over a year? I haven't touched Julie in ten months, but Pamela was very upset when she found out I gave them *both* syphilis, from earlier dalliances I enjoyed in Miami. I've said I'm sorry—twice! What's your opinion about what might be going on with her?

—Baffled and Besieged in Boca Raton

Dear Baffled,

Well, what rotten luck if your escapades gave everyone syphilis. That sort of thing can definitely throw off a marriage.

But let's consider: Could Julie have been the source of the syphilis? Maybe *she* gave it to *you*. You might want to point that out—gently—when Pamela seems calm.

Still, these violent acts of hers might be totally unrelated to your sexual adventures. As you wisely suggested, she could be bipolar, psychotic, or even schizophrenic. She might have a brain tumor. You should probably tell her to get her head examined.

If doctors find nothing, perhaps she's reliving suppressed trauma. Her own father may have broken a lamp over her head, and she forgot—until now. (Blows to the head often *cause* amnesia, you know.)

Don't rule out recurring quasi-oedipal fugue states—a fancy way of saying she might be channeling repressed feelings through a warped projection of past rage. She might be targeting you for transgressions that occurred *before you ever met!* Read that again and memorize it.

Of course, that could explain the car bomb.

Good God, man—you've got a mess on your hands. I feel for you.

Dear Advice Guru,

The wrinkled old bag who hired me as a maid last year fired me after a number of costly items went missing from her home. She screamed at me and threatened to have me arrested. I won't even speak to that witch anymore—and, in fact, I've had to move and protect myself by changing my identity.

I suffer a lot of emotional pain, but at least now I own about $40,000 worth of jewelry and household baubles, including a diamond pendant and earrings, a small Picasso, and several Lalique decanters. Here's my dilemma: I could sell it all and help my niece and younger cousin with their tuition at Texas A&M, or I could safeguard my own future by investing in the stock market. A third idea is to treat myself to some wonderful ocean cruises.

What do you suggest?
—Undecided in Daytona Beach

Dear Unindicted,

Tell your relations they should work their way through college—it'll build character. Make clear there's no shame in flipping burgers or washing cars.

You've worked hard, apparently, for a real shrew. Now live it up! A world cruise is an excellent idea. Or trek through Africa. I would give special thought to touring China, Namibia, the United Arab Emirates, or Bahrain. There's a very cool tree in Bahrain. None of those nations has an extradition agreement with the United States. Once we publish your letter, that could be a real advantage to you.

Dear Advice Guru,

I'm forty-nine years old. I'm a lifelong thumb sucker. In the past, I've coated my thumb with ham glaze, barbecue sauce, or a thin dusting of cocoa powder to improve the flavor; however, after a short while, it always goes back to the same basic, boring "skin" taste it's always had.

That aside, my deep personal anguish involves a woman at my church. I usually sit in the same pew with her, and I've seen her taking money *out* of the collection plate, even though she should be giving. Judging by her clothes and jewelry, she doesn't need the cash—she is *loaded*. A month ago, I followed her outside and noticed she drives a very expensive-looking, late-model Aston Martin.

I would very much like to ask her out. The problem is, she's married—and I also know my wife would absolutely hit the freakin' roof. What should I do?

—Lusting in Lakeview Terrace

Dear Lusting,

The anguish you mention is understandable. I put this thorny (horny?) matter to several members of my advisory board, and we reached no consensus.

The obstacles—her husband, your wife, and church decorum—are considerable. But it sounds like she's one hot babe—and rich besides. An opportunity like this may only come around once or twice in a lifetime. Sit around twiddling your thumbs—or sucking them—and it could slip away forever. Then how will you feel?

I say go for it. Worst case: her husband murders you. Or your wife murders you. But if you're truly dead, will you even care?

And since you're a churchgoer, maybe you'll shoot straight up to Heaven. Who knows?

Far more likely, you won't be murdered at all. Lots of people blow up their marriages with boneheaded acts of foolishness—and life goes on. You seem like you can handle such a bump in the road. A date with this money-filching vixen might be fun—and the memories might last a lifetime.

Dear Advice Guru,

Please tell me if I've suffered a "plastic surgery nightmare." I've seen that term online, and I'm worried it applies to me.

About a year ago, I decided to get some work done—my eyes, a facelift. I never liked my nose much (it had a bump and a knoblike shape), so I wanted that fixed too. Plus some liposuction in my cheeks and, probably the most needed, chin augmentation. My lips? I won't even describe what they looked like.

The surgeon was a man from Chechnya who said he could do it all in one day and I'd be "looking like Grace Kelly," even though I don't really know who that is. Unless Grace Kelly was in a horror movie, I don't think it worked. My eyes now look like red peepholes. My nose has an even bigger bump with a red-tipped point that lights up when I eat calamari. My lips look like fake plastic Halloween lips. My chin is twice the size it was—like he implanted a golf ball in there. Goddamn it, the quack. I got some compensation from the blithering idiot, but I wonder: Should I try again, maybe with a doctor who's not from Chechnya, or would I be risking an even *worse* plastic surgery nightmare? I'm desperate for your guidance.

—Messed Up in Malaga Cove

Dear Messed Up,

Evidently, you looked horrid before, and you look a fright now. What's the difference?

I regard plastic surgery as a roll of the dice. What you describe certainly sounds like snake eyes. Red peephole snake eyes. Bummer—but hey, maybe you still have your health, and you got a nice chunk of change from the legal settlement. Why blow it on trying to look like a dead film star?

Cut your losses. Splurge on a vacation. Go bar-hopping in some exotic locale. Just avoid the calamari hors d'oeuvres.

If you're in a gambling mood, go to Vegas. Plunk all the settlement cash on the roulette table. Lay it all on red—and let me know how it turns out.

Insults May Vary: Verbal Attacks for Any Occasion

Loathe your boss? Despise your neighbor? Regret marrying that lazy, good-for-nothing bum or that bitchy, insufferable shrew? Perhaps you've endured all that you can take, but circumstances prevent you from raising hell about it.

Never fear—Bite Me Services can help. Our seasoned attack dogs will blast any target of your choice with the ultimate in verbal abuse.* We guarantee your anonymity and complete satisfaction. Trust your righteous outrage to the very best! Visit our website today: wwv.bitemeyousickfuk.com/verbalwarfare/weeklyspecials

***Insults may vary.**

A Sampling of Recent Cases:

TARGET: Milo DeGlauzen, Winter Haven, Fla., ex-boyfriend of Tanya Marsh.

[Delivered via voicemail.]

"Hey, Milo, you don't know me, but I've seen your act—I've been following you for a good while now—and I just wanted to reach out and say what a worthless sack of donkey excrement you are. Hoo boy, you really stink, you puke-breath turd.

I'd say it right to your face, except for the stench of being around you—I'd probably vomit. I can't stand losers. I've known some big-time losers, Milo, but you set the all-time record. You should tattoo it on your forehead: *LOSER.* Tattoo it in red capital letters. Idiots like you shouldn't be allowed on the street.

You should have to wear a dunce cap as a warning to the general public. Seriously, it's hard to imagine a bigger moron. From what I hear, you've got the brains of a bowling ball. I'd bet there are smarter cockroaches. Do me a favor—don't ever get an IQ test. You might be the first air-headed freak ever held scoreless. Goodbye."

RESPONSE (if any):

[via voicemail]

"You're right, fuckhead, I don't know you—and I'm certainly glad for that. If I ever find out who you are, I'll beat the living crap out of you."

TARGET: Peggy Westerly, President of Albatross Electrical Oscillators, Inc., Spokane, Wash.

[Delivered via text message.]

"Dear Peg, just a note to acknowledge the utter incompetence you've shown driving a once-great American company into the toilet. What a fiasco! In your bumbling hands, Albatross Electrical has gone spiraling downward like a tired old seabird hit by lightning. No—make that machine-gun fire.

I can see the feathers from Mt. Hood. The corpse is in a million pieces.

Not to alarm you, but the word is out. It's all over town how you fired the one decent manager you had—poor old Kennilworth—and promoted the clueless human deadwood Haskins. That zombie's last decent idea was at least sixteen years ago.

I swear, you've got your head so far up your ass, you can

Insults May Vary

probably count the spots on your liver. Keep counting, witch. And when you're done, just fuck off and die."

RESPONSE (if any):
[via text]
"Fuck off and die *yourself*, you potty-mouth assbite piece of shit!

Who are you?! When I get my machine gun, you're the freak that's going to be in a million pieces!"

TARGET: Calvin Garrity, owner of Cal's Foreign Auto Body & Transmission Service, Tucson, Ariz.

[Delivered via voicemail.]

"Yo, Calvin, you'll never guess who this is. Just another face in the crowd of cheated, price-gouged, mad-enough-to-see-you-hang ex-customers. You've got about one chance in ten thousand to figure out which one.

Here's a clue: My sleek and pricey Italian import is now knocking and grinding like a garbage disposal chewing wingnuts—and it stalls out at every fucking stop sign. I couldn't sell it for fifty bucks and a pack of smokes.

Since you bluntly refused to address the issue, and since I haven't got the funds for a protracted legal battle, I've enlisted a Navajo medicine man to curse you from now until your dying day—which I hope is no later than next Friday.

If you're crushed by a falling engine block, that's too good for you—and you can thank my Navajo friend for the leniency. Expect worse, you chiseler.

My first dire wish was that a rabid chupacabra rip out your mother-freakin' throat. Then I thought: maybe that's too quick. Maybe you should be carried off by a thunderbird—the giant bird, not the car—kicking and screaming in horror, and finally dropped in the godforsaken desert to succumb to heat, thirst, and hopefully a mind-boggling number of rattlesnake bites.

May the Great Spirit stuff your pathetic, shriveled soul into a sealed barrel and hurl it over the south rim of the Grand Canyon."

RESPONSE (if any):

[via voicemail]

"Listen, punk—whoever you are—I don't see your number in our files. You probably got me mixed up with Lyle McCann's Saab dealership over on Denley Street.

Sue that fucker if you're going to sue anyone.

Let me tell you this, though, you sick brain-dead lunatic: You come snooping around here with your peyote and your feather-headed medicine man, I've got a barrel waiting just for you—two of them, in fact. Staring at you from my Browning shotgun.

I'll have you leaking oil from the top of your empty skull down to your bloody big toes. I'll cut off your dipstick and throw it in the junkyard.

Stick that in your peace pipe and smoke it!"

TARGET: Cassidy Haywood-Teegarden, estranged wife of Thomas L. (Tommy) Teegarden, Biloxi, Miss.

[Via registered U.S. mail]

"God damn it all to hell, Cassie, you stupid, sick, spoiled slut!

It's a beautiful blessing to me that we've never met, because I'm sure if I knew you, I would hate you with every ounce of my being. I met your husband—a wonderful, wonderful man—and he told me the story of how you've tortured him, ripped his very heart out over the past nine years, and I couldn't help but feel motivated to write this letter and tell you what a despicable, horrid, ball-breaking sociopath you are.

Insults May Vary

Tommy begged me not to write this, but hell, I'm doing it anyway—I'm so pissed off. Like I told Tommy, *'You're a broken man because of that bitch,'* and I'm guessing that if I write this letter (I was glad to do it!), it won't violate the restraining order you've got against him—which I gather was unfairly granted anyway by a corrupt, thick-headed judge, a bastard clearly biased in your favor during your ludicrous divorce action.

Tommy says he's done discussing you, he'll just move on—but I know he must have questions, lots of them. First of all: Biloxi, Mississippi? What in Christ's name are you doing in Biloxi, of all the godforsaken armpits of the world? Tommy says it took him seven months to track you down. So, Tallahassee isn't good enough for you?

I swear, you must've lost your freakin' mind, based on what Tommy told me. You should see him—heartbroken, determined to find work, still missing you despite you being such a malicious, evil wench. Cruel beyond words. Ignorant to the extreme. Cold, thoughtless ice queen.

Tommy's become a good friend of mine. I told him he should just shack up with Laura—he's practically living with her anyway. Or go after Julie, who's smart and fun and a runner-up two years ago in the Miss Florida pageant. She's made it clear she wants him. They've had some real fun together, if you know what I mean.

I'll never understand why Tommy still thinks about you, but I guess he does. My personal opinion—again, based purely on what he's confided to me—is that he's lucky you're gone.

My feeling is that you should be stood up naked in a public stockade and given a good going-over with a bullwhip for all the psychological abuse you've put that poor man through. You should be beheaded, actually. They should shoot your severed head high into the black skies over Biloxi and explode it on the Fourth of July. *Blammo!"*

RESPONSE (if any):

Attorney Robert K. Wylie filed a motion with U.S. Magistrate Judge Terrence J. Ryckoff, accusing Thomas Teegarden and his proxies—i.e., Bite Me Services—of authoring the letter in violation of a lawful restraining order. Teegarden was remanded into custody to serve a six-month jail sentence. Bite Me was stripped of its license to do business in the state of Florida, with a similar action now pending in Mississippi.

TARGET: Dennis M. Logan, Vice President of the Maripol District Homeowners Assn., Rancho Cucamonga, Calif.

[Via direct phone conversation on a recorded line}

Bite Me agent: "There you are, you fuckhead. You imbecile. You feckless scourge upon humanity."

Dennis: "Who is this?"

Bite Me agent: "I'm the guy about to sue your sorry ass, so listen up, fish-breath."

Dennis: "Sue me? Tone down the gratuitous rancor and tell me for what."

Bite Me agent: "It's a long list. Stupidity should be the main cause of action, plus brazen hypocrisy. And the fact that you're just plain ugly. You should be shelling out millions on the ugly charge alone."

Dennis: "I won't tolerate this type of crap. You've got about thirty seconds to—"

Bite Me agent: "Just shut your pie-hole and take notes, dickwad. You mentally deranged ignoramus."

Dennis: "Ten seconds. Tell me what you want, asshole!"

Bite Me agent: "What I want? Let's start with jamming a red-hot poker up your bloated keister. That would make me happy. God, yes, that would take some air out of your balloon, wouldn't it, Mr. HOA Rules and Regulations?"

Insults May Vary

Dennis: "You got a beef with the HOA? I don't make the rules, moron!"

Bite Me agent: "Oh, but you love to crack down, don't you, Mr. Hypocrite? Hand out fines, and meanwhile you've got your stereo going at ten at night, blasting out your open windows—Barry Manilow, John Denver, Zamfir and that fucking pan flute."

Dennis: "Is this Carl Goetz?"

Bite Me agent: "Strike one, monkey face. No—I won't insult the monkeys. You're more like a warthog with acne. Sheesh, man, shave that caterpillar off your lip!"

Dennis: "Is this about Carl and that car on his lawn?"

Bite Me agent: "Let's talk about the hours you run your sprinklers."

Dennis: "Peggy McAllister? You're calling for Peggy, aren't you? I consider her to be insane. I'm done dealing with her—nor will I put up with any hired goons such as yourself adding misery to my life. I've got enough!"

Bite Me agent: "You're about to get more."

Dennis: "The hell I am. The rules are clear—no pink houses! Tell that mentally deranged, obsessive-repulsive psychopath that we allow earth tones only. A wide range of them. No pink, no lilac, no fuchsia, no polka dots or candy-cane stripes. Tell her to cease and desist already!"

Bite Me agent: "You don't have a clue, do you? I don't even know a Peggy."

Dennis: "You're lucky. Count your blessings."

Bite Me agent: "I will wreck your life."

Dennis: "Lon Walters?!"

Bite Me agent: "Nice try, Bozo. You must have a fungus growing in your brain. You're about to go through serious changes, you ugly, fat, Nazi tyrant."

Dennis: "You'll regret this, fuckhead. Connie Lanzano? Did she put you up to this?"

Bite Me agent: "Wrong again. You'll be hearing from my former CIA assassin. Goodbye."

RESPONSE (if any):

For a substantial additional fee, Bite Me Services assigned a professional thug to travel to Rancho Cucamonga and "give Dennis Logan the what-for."

The thug hid in the shadows of the parking lot outside Everly's Bar & Grill and met Dennis with a forceful roundhouse punch to the nose.

In subsequent weeks, motor vehicles belonging to Carl Goetz, Peggy McAllister, Lon Walters, and Connie Lanzano were firebombed in the wee hours of the morning. Peggy also claimed she was shot in the buttocks by a BB gun.

Police say an investigation is ongoing.

Novel Flops: Unpublished Sequels of the Literary Giants

Imagine having a terrible case of shingles and feeling like your skin is on fire—or having your skin actually catch fire, which results in the same sort of horrific burning sensation. OK, now imagine a root canal gone awry. Mother-freakin' pain like you can't believe. Or an excruciating back spasm at the top of the stairs that causes you to pitch forward, arms windmilling, and tumble all the way to the hard concrete floor of your basement.

Ask any author—these agonies are easily preferable to the psychological torment of having a manuscript rejected. A novel, say, that required years of toil, an arduous accumulation of intellectual labor meted out through the lonely, monotonous tap-tap-tapping of a keyboard. The risk of such a failure prompts many writers—even great ones—to follow the triumphant publication of one novel (if the miracle should happen) with a related story: a sequel. One that, by offering a similar title, exploits a lucrative, ready-made market.

The stratospheric rise of J.K. Rowling illustrates the point. Though armed with a wonderful literary idea involving a Taiwanese orphan who bobs for apples along the seacoast, Rowling churned out her second *Harry Potter* tale instead—putting herself (and her publishing house) on a path to riches.

Sadly, though, and far too often, even towering giants of letters have seen this strategy backfire. When the intended sequel is an obvious dud—so audaciously flawed it would sully the writer's reputation forever—astute agents and editors scramble to sweep every last wrongheaded noun and participle under the literary rug. It's as if the colossal misfire was never written.

Substantial snooping was required to detail these examples:

Love in the Time of Epilepsy, by Gabriel García Márquez

Only a freakish uptick in the popularity of third-world pestilence—both as a literary topic and as a challenge for the millions of sick and dying—enabled Márquez to publish his blockbuster, *Love in the Time of Cholera*. The sequel soured early on when he chose to build the narrative around the epileptic seizures experienced by his forty-nine-year-old cousin Cristobal during his romantic pursuit of the teen vamp Maria next door.

"I'm afraid I must point out a flaw in the underlying premise, my dear friend," Márquez's publisher objected. "Given that epilepsy is not a communicable disease, it can't be said to have 'a time' in the fashion of a normal epidemic. It lacks the grave urgency and gravitas of a cholera outbreak."

Stung, Márquez wrote back, *"It's always a time of epilepsy for the epileptic!"*—an argument he abruptly abandoned, apparently in a moment of epiphany. He then embarked on a furious, year-long period of revision.

The result: a wholly restructured, thematically overhauled six-hundred-page opus, *Love in the Time of Beriberi*. Dark, complex, and often disjointed, the new story felt "utterly devoid of hope," Márquez admitted. Every key character died. He then did one final about-face, combining misery, pathos, and sarcastic humor in a claustrophobic psychological thriller, *Love in the Time of Whooping Cough*.

One editor described it as "abysmal." Márquez subsequently bound all three aborted manuscripts into a weighty bundle and burned them in a bonfire in the rugged mountains near his home.

Insults May Vary

The Raisins of Wrath, by John Steinbeck

Few novels of the era even approached the stark power of Steinbeck's Pulitzer Prize–winning Dust Bowl elegy, *The Grapes of Wrath*. Editors at Viking Press considered it a no-brainer that Steinbeck would further exploit the "sour grapes" theme by cranking out fruit-monikered jeremiads—*The Grapefruits of Grievance, The Apples of Anarchy, The Kumquats of Discontent*, etc.

The Sue Grafton–esque series, before Grafton was even Grafton, might have cemented Steinbeck's redoubtable legacy. Alas, he and Viking clashed over their visions for sequel No. 1.

The strong-willed author hoped to continue the saga of the penurious Joad family as they adapted to new, more-exciting lives in California. Turned off by "grapefruit," and notoriously incapable of writing without a title firmly in mind, Steinbeck pushed hard to call the new book *The Beverly Hillbillies*—a title later appropriated by TV executives.

Editors fought back with an array of alternatives, eventually favoring the alliteration afforded by *Raisins*. They also insisted the Joads open one of L.A.'s first surf shops, where they would sell reefer on the sly to Hollywood stars.

Steinbeck balked. His writing began to suffer. He couldn't spell words with R, W, or A in them. He spent days angrily pounding typewriter keys at random.

Scholars still debate whether he quit or was fired from his contract.

The Battery-Operated Kool-Aid Vending Machine, by Tom Wolfe

A trailblazing dandy with a gift for garb, Wolfe skyrocketed to fame in part by profiling maverick hippie-author Ken Kesey and his Merry Pranksters in *The Electric Kool-Aid Acid Test*. What isn't

David Ferrell

widely remembered is that Wolfe had been, coincidentally, a heavy Kool-Aid drinker during his own childhood—and he saw enormous pop-culture significance in the sugary, fruit-flavored beverage.

Swayed by Kesey, Wolfe set aside other assignments to explore Kool-Aid's various and sometimes insidious influences on the 1960s. During a road trip through Bend, Oregon, Wolfe happened upon a gas station vending machine that dispensed nothing but Kool-Aid. No colas or root beer. No 7-Up. Just Kool-Aid.

The eye-catching machine featured a revolving neon sign and was powered by two standard automobile batteries. Wolfe found station owner Oscar Givens to be "a fascinating wack job," a former zinc miner and railroad brakeman who had done time for running a numbers racket in Idaho.

In what proved a creative mistake, Wolfe attempted to craft the story as both a history of Idaho and an exposé of the U.S. vending machine industry.

"It was schizophrenic—too this and too that," said one editor who rejected the 900-page abomination. "It certainly didn't help that Wolfe wanted every third word to be in ALL CAPS."

The Old Lady on the Bus, by Paula Hawkins

In her contemporary thriller *The Girl on the Train*, Hawkins mesmerized readers with the story of a young woman who witnessed an apparent crime from a train window. The "non-sequel sequel" sought to stand alone as an "up-close, in-your-face kind of drama," according to one publishing insider.

The heroine this time was a dour, asthmatic octogenarian, Lucy Ann Crabbe, who commuted on Bus No. 94 in Albuquerque to her job at a local senior center. Rather than glimpse a single shocking event outside the window, Crabbe saw—through a cloud of cataracts and scratched eyeglasses—a veritable plethora of unsettling sights *inside* the bus.

She watched a ninety-year-old passenger get knocked around

by a purse thief. She noticed that the afternoon driver had a habit of sneaking swigs from a suspicious brown travel mug—very likely booze.

Individually, none of the observations were earth-shaking, but the novel shrewdly marshaled a long accumulation of tiny, ambiguous events to stir legitimate concern for Crabbe's mental well-being. Here was a woman already taking mood stabilizers, for godsakes.

The buzz in literary circles was that Hawkins might attempt yet another rewrite—perhaps eliminating the tedious itemized lists of Albuquerque streets, bus routes, and convenience stores.

Portnoy's Legal Action, by Philip Roth

Mixed in with all the acclaim for *Portnoy's Complaint* were plenty of barbs aimed at the lascivious Alexander Portnoy, Roth's maladjusted narrator. "What a crybaby!" one reviewer scoffed. "If Mr. Portnoy is that screwed up, he should spend more time with the head-shrinker and stop the belly-aching."

Stung by such feedback, Roth devoted eleven years to crafting the sequel, in which Portnoy finally sheds his victimhood, hires an attorney, and mounts a courtroom attack. The titular "legal action" refers to a civil suit filed against his parents, seeking $500 million in damages for gross incompetence and emotional neglect during his upbringing.

That was just the beginning. The manuscript chronicled dozens of lawsuits filed by the ever-more-vindictive Portnoy, a vexatious litigant of the first order. He even goes after his psychoanalyst, Dr. Spielvogel—a new wrinkle in the story reveals the shrink was a former tuna-boat captain who forged his therapist credentials in order to meet women with abnormal sexual cravings.

The plot's escalating complexity ultimately thwarted Roth's expectations of being published.

"Take this manuscript home," he was advised, "and on a cold

winter's night, shove it into your furnace."

Which, supposedly, he did—proclaiming it a "really hot novel" as the pages curled up in flame.

Roosevelt in the Bathroom, by George Saunders

From the poignant, atmospheric milieu of his award-winning *Lincoln in the Bardo*, Saunders leapt forward by an apropos four score years to delve into the private anguish of another presidential luminary: Franklin Delano Roosevelt.

Both leaders were burdened by war. Lincoln's deeper sorrow involved the death of his young son. Roosevelt, too, suffered—but in ways the public never saw. Mainly, polio. FDR had a hell of a time, in his stricken state, navigating the cramped White House bathrooms. It was all he could do to reach a new roll of toilet paper from a seated position on the commode.

True to *Bardo* form, Saunders compressed the action even further—detailing, in 630 manuscript pages, a span of just twenty-five minutes on a May night in 1941.

The wild and woolly narrative—was it dark comedy?—offered a vivid glimpse of the harried president, left alone (his usual attendants were out sick), trying to squeeze in a bathroom break before dinner with his Cabinet. The world was in chaos. Hitler had taken France. Greece and Yugoslavia had been crushed by the Nazi blitzkrieg. The Luftwaffe was bombing London.

And Roosevelt—ever self-conscious about personal grooming—couldn't seem to locate his fingernail clippers.

They weren't in the drawer where he'd left them. In a fateful twist, a new housekeeper had rearranged everything in an attempt to bring order to the chaos. FDR's frustrated shouting, banging, and painful lurching as he searched for the clippers—finally located in a box in the medicine cabinet—formed a wrenching counterpoint to the burned roast in the dining room.

Saunders' yarn exhibited his usual strong stylistic touches. Publishers, though, found the action predictable. *Of course* Roosevelt was upset. And it felt unseemly to blame the poor housekeeper, a nonpartisan civil servant and a vast improvement over the last incompetent nitwit.

For Whom the Phone Rings, by Ernest Hemingway

"Rick, it's for you. Something about an investment opportunity."

So begins Hemingway's rollicking sequel to *For Whom the Bell Tolls*, his acclaimed novel of the Spanish Civil War. Though thrilled by the original's success, Hemingway was tired of writing about armed conflict.

"War, war, war—it's nothing but violence," he complained.

He set the new story in the comparative paradise of Key West, Florida, where he had been living—and where, incidentally, there was an excellent seafood restaurant called The Starfish.

His protagonists: Rick "Tricky Ricky" Ellis, a former mercenary now home from the Spanish conflict and slinging drinks at the Starfish Lounge; and Bettina Curtis, a saucy, red-haired siren working as a switchboard operator. The tempestuous relationship between Rick and Bettina became the crux of a wry novel packed with steamy subplots, watery graves, and dry martinis.

When Rick dropped her—thanks to post-war anxiety and a comely young tart named Rachel—Bettina hatched a plan. First, a pipe bomb. Then, when that felt too risky, she pursued revenge by other means: transferring a barrage of bizarre, goofy "wrong-number" calls to Rick's private line, night after night.

The 99th such incident sent Rick into a spiral of comic rage.

Hemingway had high hopes for the dark romp, calling it "a brave tale, an honest tale, and most of all, a cautionary tale."

But the book's chances were doomed when half of the manuscript (the only copy) blew away in Hurricane Cassandra.

David Ferrell

Innocent Bystander Dead: A 'Blind Assassin' Novel, by Margaret Atwood

Clearly high on the oohs and aahs from *The Blind Assassin*, Atwood appeared to be gunning for another Man Booker Prize when she cooked up a sequel every bit as harrowing—and at least twice as convoluted.

The original work featured a story within a story within a story. The sequel? Six stories, nested like cursed Matryoshka dolls.

At the center again: a raucous yarn about a sightless hitman, Lewis, who roamed the streets of Toronto, hellbent on gunning down a mysterious financier known only as "Mr. M." The task might have been easier had he ever managed to learn Mr. M's full name. As it was, Lewis mistakenly blew away a hapless hotel doorman named Gary Lemieux.

The shooting was "only a fictional story," we're told, within nested story No. 2. But in nested story No. 5, we learn that Lemieux was a real person—except his name was actually Witherspoon—and he wasn't a hapless doorman after all; he was a jewel thief and corporate spy for the sinister pharmaceutical firm Zilneth.

That's the same Zilneth whose CEO, it turns out, was raping and abusing his kindly French wife—the narrator of story No. 3.

Ultimately, Lemieux/Witherspoon—the supposedly real guy—gets shot again anyway, this time by a bank robber in story No. 4, suggesting that a violent death might have been the poor bastard's fate no matter what.

Someone else gets shot, too. That might change in the rewrite.

Coming to bookstores soon. Maybe.

Who Else Is Afraid of Virginia Woolf?, by Edward Albee

If the erudite Ms. Woolf could frighten one poor soul, surely she would intimidate other intellectual poseurs, too. That was no great logical leap for master playwright Edward Albee, who intended to follow his Tony Award-winning hit with yet another foray into acrimonious relationships.

Where did he go wrong?

Perhaps this theatrical sequel was too ribald, too abstruse, too laced with scientific jargon and highbrow set pieces. Every principal character was a published physicist or a Mensa board member. Critic Rosalind Epperfeld, who was given a copy of the unproduced play, called it "a fast cure for insomnia."

"Science is great. Love science. Love literature. Love ancient Babylonian history," she said. "But are we really supposed to sit through twenty minutes of analysis of the Schrödinger wave equation? And tedious critiques of Woolf's prose style? No thank you!"

To his credit—perhaps—Albee conceded that his aim was "too high over the heads of the ignorant masses."

"Let's face it," he added, "most people are dolts. The idiots took over the planet a long time ago, and they don't appear willing to give it up."

Few argued. But still he wasted a hell of a lot of time.

Slaughterhouse Six, by Kurt Vonnegut

First Billy Pilgrim became unstuck in time. Now—voilà!—he's unstuck in space. Bouncing here, there, back and forth, flitting between realities as if in a glitchy video game.

One moment, the shell-shocked Billy is at home in his kitchen, spreading brie on a cracker. The next—*pooooofff!*—he's in the men's room of Slaughterhouse Six, a hangar-like structure that, long after the war, has been converted into artist lofts.

How did he get there? Was he searching for an abstract-expressionist landscape to hang above the fireplace? Or just lost?

Billy's confusion didn't matter, because seconds later—boom—he was in a dentist's chair, mouth stuffed with cotton, enduring a root canal.

Vonnegut, ever the audacious rule-breaker, saw a chance to cut loose—and indulge his not-so-latent sadistic streak—by tormenting his psychologically tattered antihero in a barely cohesive ramble. This fraught mosaic of disconnected vignettes lacked the underlying thematic thread that held *Slaughterhouse-Five* together.

And yes—there was an actual train wreck on page 298. A fiery one. What to make of the grisly collision, and Billy disembarking through a hole in spacetime only seconds before the Big Bang?

Cosmic? Sure. Believable? *No way, Jose!*

Suddenly, Billy is safe in a booth at the Dresden Grill, about to bite into a kraut dog. A blink later, he's in an airport line in Los Angeles, watching TSA agents confiscate his mouthwash.

"Just yanking Billy's chain—that was Vonnegut's sole mission," said one Random House editor. "It was an unreadable mess. Just like *Slaughterhouses One through Four*."

***None Dare Call It Cowardice*, by John A. Stormer**

The literary waters were rarely calm for the aptly named John A. Stormer. His florid 1964 anti-communist screed, *None Dare Call It Treason*, brought immediate (and rather ironic) accusations of treason from liberal intellectuals.

Outrage doesn't cover Stormer's reaction. He was "literally foaming at the mouth," recalled one friend.

Intent on revenge, Stormer began work on a sequel—a rapscallion's broad sword to the thick heads of his critics. Yet he made several egregious literary blunders.

The first? A ninety-page essay on the very *meaning* of cowardice. At first, he extolled it as "the better part of valor." Later, he declared it "a chickenshit way to be."

Then came the characters—thinly veiled celebrity stand-ins who had dared insult him in public. Humphrey Bogart was one. A known defender of blacklisted screenwriters, Bogart appeared in Stormer's narrative as *Humberto Boogard-Smith*, a "creepy little wiseguy" who "somehow snared a lead role in *Casablanca*."

Boogard-Smith was portrayed as being afraid of his own shadow.

One widely circulated (and possibly apocryphal) story claims Bogart ran into Stormer one night outside Chasen's in L.A. and punched both of the author's eyes to the color of uncooked eggplant.

Another Freakin' Bunch of Mistakes!, by Jonathan Franzen

Implicit in this sequel to his earlier masterwork *The Corrections* was the desperate pursuit of order. Things got fixed—finally! But now . . . what the hell?

Oh, for the love of God.

That was the essence of Franzen's suffocatingly maudlin follow-up, a restless 800-page saga tracing the Lambert family's continued descent into dysfunction.

Unfortunately, what unfolded was a relentless parade of new missteps: larceny, bank fraud, sexual assault, and domestic terrorism. These weren't just family squabbles. It felt as though this troupe of harebrained sociopaths had devoted themselves to dismantling modern America.

At one point, Gary, the eldest sibling, booby-trapped a New York subway track with landmines—causing a massive explosion that launched a homeless man over a berm and into the East River.

Realizing the novel was an unsalvageable misfire, Franzen admitted he "just needed to work out some residual angst." Soon after, he began work on his next (grandly received) bestseller: *Freedom*.

David Ferrell

Gobsmacked to a Fair Farthing (and Other Exciting New Cliches)

It might sound impertinent to say, but our language is running out of steam. Think about it: We rely a lot—some would say too much—on the humble cliché, a staple of modern expression and the most sure-fire means of telling it like it is. While cliches are hugely important—they do much of the heavy lifting both in speech and literature—lately far too many are sounding trite, too same-old, same-old. Even the phrase tired old cliché has itself become a tired old cliché.

Not to beat a dead horse, but this sad fact threatens to erode the rich descriptive legacy of our culture. It feels personal to me. Early in my writing career, clichés were my bread and butter. Lately I've come to avoid them like the plague, which is a crying shame. Every time I sit down at the keyboard, I'm forced to re-invent the wheel, linguistically speaking.

Thankfully (I know you'll thank me), I've gone back to the intellectual drawing board, so to speak, and developed a laundry list of pithy, vibrant new clichés to supplant some of the old duds that are fading out. Here they are, below. All I ask is that you properly credit me if you find yourself tossing out one of these delectable morsels to great effect at a cocktail party, or if you slip one or more (or even a bunch!) into that new novel or screenplay you're writing. Aside from this small courtesy, there is no charge—they're free!

Insults May Vary

The full list:

Like a monkey changing diapers —
Don't forget that in scientific experiments, monkeys perform generally worse than even young white-collar professionals at the task of changing diapers. In fact, if there happens to a fan in the room, something is sure to hit it, calling to mind another familiar cliché. This expression, then, suggests an overblown, lost-all-control sort of disorder. It can be used as a simile and also metaphorically, to wit: "That quack can't do surgery. He's a monkey changing diapers in the operating room."

A hairball down the gullet —
Let's face it, every meal is a crapshoot, unless you always order corn flakes in almond milk. If the goal is culinary rapture, you might achieve it with a cheesy slice of pizza. Less lucky, you could wind up in the emergency room for graciously devouring Aunt Mindy's chicken tetrazzini or her strange-smelling shellfish concoction in clam sauce. Imagine you're having your stomach pumped—or, no, let's say you're merely genuflecting throughout the long, miserable night before the toilet god, wishing you were dead. How do you even begin to describe the ordeal? Short of saying, "The witch tried to poison me," you might offer the sharp but understated comment, "It was a hairball down the gullet." This versatile condemnation can be applied with equal vigor to badly prepared lamb shank, lasagna, matzo balls or quiche lorraine—or, in fact, to any unpleasant experience metaphorically jammed down your throat, like a history report on the Mayans or a mandatory trip to driving school.

David Ferrell

Gobsmacked to a fair farthing —

It's Valentine's Day and you present your beloved with a fancy fruit-and-nut loaf in a colorful tin; in return, you're handed divorce papers. Or picture yourself in the boss's office, hopeful of finally moving up. Except you're hit with the news that the job and the hefty raise have gone to the creepy a-hole from accounts receivable. No banal declamation about being "shocked" or "upset" carries nearly the punch of proclaiming, "I was gobsmacked to a fair farthing." The anachronistic tenor alone serves to brand yourself as the social misfit, the lone wolf, that you truly are. Keep in mind it is one thing to be gobsmacked; it is quite another to be gobsmacked to a fair farthing. Was there a time, perhaps in the days of Sir Galahad, when this potent cliche was as commonplace as "cat's pajamas" and "pig in a poke"? If so, it is long overdue to be brought back and ably exploited.

Disasterique du jour —

As the briny sea bard Jacques Cousteau so rightly pointed out, French aristocratic phrases, whether old or new, evoke a certain nom de fleur, and must always be used correctly or else you look like an idiot. Du jour, signifying "mediocre at best" or "extremely commonplace," is, of course, well known to most Americans because of the widely emulated cook-book jargon of yesteryear: soup du jour being a hopelessly average soup no matter where you get it, especially if they throw in chunks of potato, so don't let the prices fool you! The nascent cliché disasterique du jour describes a disaster of routine or commonplace dimensions; i.e., "the usual mess," a SNAFU; a.k.a., a fucking mess or a fucking SNAFU or fucking disaster, sometimes written as a FUCKING DISASTER or GODDAMNED SHIT SHOW, and frequently combined with various other epithets, hurled invectives, rants, tantrums, personal threats and ugly blasphemies.

A bran muffin to you, then! —

A hearty, life-affirming salutation, normally extended from one good friend to another. Besides symbolizing robust health, the bran muffin connotes discipline—you could be wolfing down a Ding Dong, right?—and hints vaguely at a persistent problem with cholesterol. Thus, "A bran muffin to you, then" implicitly acknowledges the over-arching yin and yang of consumption and abstinence, abundance and desperation. While unapologetically intimate in nature, this cliche, when properly elocuted by men of a resolutely manly bearing, rings with a hail masculinity that is perhaps best described as Hemingway-esque. Shout it from a distance—across a busy boulevard, for example—like Bogart or John Wayne. Like Brando on the waterfront. The greeting can be bellowed, snorted, rasped, uttered or called out in full throaty volume with a merry twinkle in the eye. In a test case, it was used mockingly in response to an insult. "Hey, Phillip, you're looking fatter every day!" "Oh, yeah? A bran muffin to you, then, asshole!"

God in His underpants —

This powerful utterance refers to the real truth, unadorned by hyperbole or extraneous embellishment. Is God wearing jeans and spats? No. Is the Almighty preening in some white ruffled shirt or trying to look beachy and cool in one of those Abercrombie & Fitch patterned Oxfords with navy-blue cords and striped rubber flip-flops? No—God no! He is just being God, stripped down to the basics. The Big Guy being real—and you'd better like it. "God in His underpants knows I didn't run the stop sign," you might tell a traffic officer. Or, while haggling with your television provider: "No, I never ordered Pay-Per-View, I swear to God in His underpants!"

Stick one up yer gerdalnik —

A bravura addition to the long line of "stick one up" clichés that have proven so popular over the years. This fresh take heightens the impact, bringing an element of surprise to the invective. The original offender is likely to think, "Yer gerdalnik? What's he talking about?" And the joke will be on him. He thinks he's missed something. He feels foolish, ignorant, possibly stupid—which, let's face it, he might well be. Who am I to judge? But, in fact, he hasn't missed anything. Yer gerdalnik has no meaning! The confusion you've engendered may lodge in your adversary's mind all day, or all week, stuck in his craw, as it were—like a poppyseed jammed between the molars. Like a hairball down the gullet, if you like. Smile and applaud yourself. You've jumped a critical step ahead in the all-important psychological game.

Way too anchovy, or, Way too anchovy, dude —

With a nod to surf culture and/or the daring crews of coastal trawlers, this new cliché—meant to be voiced in a languid, California-esque slur—means simply "too damn small." It draws inspiration from the puny size of the saltwater fish and can be applied to anything from waves at the jetty to hamburgers, pay raises, or reproductive organs. Caution is advised: the phrase is easy to misinterpret. "That pizza is way too anchovy" says nothing about the presence of anchovies. It simply observes that the horde will go hungry because cheapskate Dad wouldn't spring for a large.

Give wings to your spittle —

A defiant, exuberant exhortation. Do what thou wilt, consequences be damned. Quite literally, "Spit on anything you want"—you're in the catbird seat, pal. No nanny, no meddling mother-in-law is going to stop you. Hawk one up and let it go. Vent.

Insults May Vary

Become a fountain of righteous bodily fluids, if that suits your needs. Rain your saliva down. Seed the clouds with your thick, self-aggrandizing phlegm.

"Give wings to that spittle, old boy. Give it freakin' wings like Pegasus—and let it fly."

Mop like a top —

In this context, *mop* becomes an action verb. You're mopping the floor—it's been filthy for weeks. Crumbs. Dust. Dog hairs. And you're spinning like a top. Isn't that the predicament of much of working America? Going in circles, exhausted, but trying to make progress.

"I mopped like a top all day and I'm still not caught up. God, I need a drink."

Honking Helena's horn —

Does Helena want her horn honked? Probably not—she could easily honk it herself. But as a fresh spin on "yanking someone's chain," this zinger offers a more playful and less chauvinistic jab. Yanking a chain suggests sadism. Honking a horn? Mischievous fun. Better still, Helena doesn't even need to exist—it's just a figure of speech.

"I was totally honking Helena's horn!"

Women can reclaim the phrase by swapping in alliterative names:

"I honked Horace's horn and it was hysterical."

Trade a hen for a wombat —

Let's set aside the fact that you wouldn't want either. You've got a hen—lays eggs, maybe dinner. And you trade it... for a wombat. Big mistake. Wombats are aggressive, ill-tempered, and basically the deadbeat cousins of Australia's animal kingdom.

"What were you thinking?"

"It's a wombat!"

"Nope, get it out of here."

A wildly bad trade. A cautionary metaphor for catastrophically poor decision-making.

Turn turnips into tube socks —

Forget silk purses from sows' ears. That's passé—and silk's expensive. Turnips are cheap. So here's the modern twist: turn mundane, unwanted produce into something oddly useful and unexpected.

"Through grit and ingenuity, she turned turnips into tube socks."

It's a hat tip to improbable success—farm-to-footwear miracles in an unforgiving world.

Like a duck at the dentist —

A timely replacement for the weary "fish out of water" cliché. Our duck has left the pond, which is bad enough. Now he has the added horror of being at the dentist. And he doesn't even have any teeth.

What's he doing here?

Gum disease?

Bill trouble?

Regardless of the reason, he's clearly out of place, uncomfortable, and paying for the privilege.

"I was like a duck at the dentist the whole time—confused, anxious, and what they charged me—my God!"

Fizzy on, old seltzer—

The seltzer tablet: it fizzes . . . then it's gone. A perfect symbol for life—brief, noisy, then nothing.

To fizzy on is to endure. Hang in there. Exist with dignity as long as humanly possible, even as everything dissolves around you.

"Fizzy on, old seltzer," whispers the young boy to the frail elder sipping chicken broth near the bus depot.

"Fizzy on, dear boy. Fizzy on, all of you dear readers—fizzy on."

David Ferrell

Now It Can Be Told: One Man's Torrid Love Affair With Liz Taylor

Upon his untimely death in a fiery dune buggy crash at the age of ninety-three, Carlyle Henrik St. Pierre left behind a seaside condo housing a hoarder's trove: among his personal effects were badminton racquets, old chrome hubcaps, bags of pilfered ashtrays, wigs, leather jackets, a Super-8 movie projector, two Hula Hoops, a voodoo doll depicting former President George W. Bush (with a pin through its eye), shelves of *National Geographic* magazines, a harpoon, a xylophone, several dozen photo albums, and the following letter.

Addressed to no one and handwritten in shaky but legible script, the missive seems a confession—albeit one oozing with braggadocio. Or possibly it is a reckless boast infused with feigned Victorian guilt. No matter. The real questions remain unclear: why St. Pierre wrote it, and to whom he might have been planning to send it. That aside, the bold account may prove to be rooted wholly or partially in fact—and inasmuch as it may be of some historical interest (at least in the film world), it is reprinted here in its entirety.

(By Carlyle Henrik St. Pierre)
Shame is the most embarrassing of all emotions—with the possible exception of total embarrassment. I'm talking about the very deepest kind of shame: the shame of being swept into an illicit affair with one of Hollywood's most alluring women. The shame

of hiding, sneaking around, meeting for one clandestine rendezvous after another in sumptuous hotel suites, mountain chalets, city penthouses, and yachts. Being the plaything of a world-famous sex goddess at the frenetic apex of her beauty and celebrity.

My shame about the relationship was so profound that it kept me silent for more than half a century. I literally went decades without speaking—about anything.

This put a tremendous crimp in my social life. Friends slowly drifted away. A few said, "Fuck you, jackass," and vanished straight off. It hurt. On the plus side, I avoided a lot of boring family dinners and saved a ton on my phone bill. Still, it took a long while for my perspective to evolve. One day, it hit me like a thunderbolt: instead of feeling shame, I should feel tremendous pride.

Oops!

Yes—pride that my longtime inamorata overcame her many quirks and insecurities to make a success of herself. Pride that so many movie fans—and so many husbands—absolutely adored her. Pride that she managed to finish shooting *Cleopatra*, despite the constant distraction that I—and possibly also Richard Burton—caused her.

For sixteen blissful, exhilarating, tumultuous, downright rocky, cloudy, sunny, partly clearing, and alternately cold and very hot years, I was (yes!) Elizabeth Taylor's secret lover. The affair grabbed us like a schnauzer clamping down on a pair of bacon-scented rag dolls and shaking furiously until all the cotton stuffing flew out. It was far too powerful for either of us to control.

Liz and I met, by chance, at a produce market in London, where I pivoted rapidly with my hand-basket and knocked an eggplant from her grasp. It fell and smashed on the concrete floor. She did what any woman of her stature might do: she slapped me—hard—and then we both laughed uproariously. Right away, we could laugh with each other—and at each other.

This was in 1958, soon after the plane-crash death of Liz's third husband, Mike Todd. "Little Hoochie-Coochie-Goochie," as I came to call her, certainly needed the laughs. She was twenty-six and I was barely seventeen, skinny as a sapling but tall for my age at six-foot-seven.

Together, we rode the wild wave of ecstasy like surfers hanging ten at the Banzai Pipeline—until we plunged headlong into the churning whitewaters of regret in 1974. Fate caught up with us that year, knocking us every which way to Sunday. Liz finally kicked tired old Richard to the curb in order to be mine forever. I'd been begging her to do it—except when it happened (bad timing), I almost immediately dumped her for a flax-haired vixen I met at a Hertz counter in Baltimore. A sultry young waif who promptly tossed me aside like a dirty Kleenex two weeks later.

Regrets? I can only quote Sinatra—I've had a few. Maybe enough to fill a tanker truck. But what a ride it was! The memories are piled up like so many rocks on one of those endless New England beaches Barry Manilow sang about. Or like shells on one of those beaches that are nothing but shells.

Here's a moment: We're arm-in-arm, entering a movie theater in 1961 to see *The Misfits* with Clark Gable and Marilyn Monroe. I gently maneuver Liz toward the snack counter.

"Tootsie Roll?" I offer.

"You know I can't eat with this mask," she tells me.

Fearful of being mobbed and determined to keep our relationship out of the tabloids, Liz went out with me only while wearing a rubber Halloween mask—a dead ringer for Richard Nixon.

"You can take it off during the movie, when the lights are out," I said. This seemed to please her. I sprung for Tootsie Rolls, popcorn, and a couple of Cokes, but when the film started Liz grew fretful. She worried I would find Marilyn more attractive.

Beauty-wise, it was a dead heat. But to quell my darling's jealousy, I whispered a series of snarky remarks about Marilyn's appearance—that she looked old, kind of chubby. That she'd obviously had a hard life and wasn't aging well.

Insults May Vary

These tender favors meant an enormous amount to Liz. I saw her smile. She squeezed my hand.

Her insecurities were many, but somehow endearing. She often remarked that her toes were too long—"like white, wriggling eels poking out from the coral. Oh, I can't stand them!" she'd exclaim. Liz hired artists to paint them in pastel shades to achieve a foreshortening effect. Salvador Dalí was the best at this—when available. She had to pay him dearly. Sometimes she'd beg Dalí to paint butterflies and little elephants on her knees, because she thought her kneecaps were too plain.

Her beauty was exquisite, yet she was a bundle of contradictions. Stung by being labeled injury-prone, she grew keenly self-protective, cloaking herself in "mink" stoles actually made of foam padding. She wore a football helmet during outings, in case a stray object—a rock, a barbell—fell from a high window and conked her on the head.

And yet, Liz would defiantly go up and down stairs in roller skates, or practice fencing—her favorite sport—during electrical storms.

"Why don't you just carry a lightning rod?" I once called out the window to her.

"The foil works better!" she hollered back, cheerfully.

Long before most people ever heard of multiple personality disorder, I speculated about my poor sweet Liz. I even confronted her. At first, she agreed—claiming to be six different women, two men, and a Persian housecat named Fluffy. Later, when I pressed her to seek help, she blew up.

"Multiple personality? Are you out of your mind? How DARE you!"

The last time I raised the topic, Liz offered only a wan look and began reciting a verse from the *Bhagavad Gita*.

Though her accommodations were invariably posh, her tastes were simple during our early years together. Nothing excited her more than opening a can of Chef Boyardee cheese ravioli and dining in. Or fixing a TV dinner—usually a chicken cutlet. Occasionally the meal would be burnt due to her notorious trouble with food timers. However, Liz always insisted—and I agreed—that any mistake could be remedied with a thick dollop of mayonnaise.

After dinner, when she stayed at the Dakota in Manhattan, we would gaze out the window at the pigeons. Liz liked to speculate about whether the birds made love or just went through the motions during sex—like so many of her friends. To make her laugh, I would drop water balloons onto the crowded sidewalks below. Liz would scold me, then forgive me, then drop a balloon or two herself, guffawing like a hyena. It was probably our favorite thing to do together.

We'd also watch television for hours—*Red Skelton, Jackie Gleason,* even test patterns once it got late. She could stare at the same test pattern for three or four hours, then change the channel and watch a different one, often 'til dawn. Her chronic insomnia bored me to the point that I couldn't stay awake around her.

Lack of sleep did not slow her down. If anything, it made her more restless. One day she told me, "I'm going nuts—I need a hobby. I want to start a collection."

"A collection of what?" I asked.

"Little ceramic polar bears," she said. "Or matchbook covers. Or maybe swizzle sticks. You think swizzle sticks are interesting? I have one from the Waldorf."

We talked for a long while about swizzle sticks and miniature birds and penguins. Finally, I said, "What about jewelry?"

"Jewelry?"

"Why not diamonds?" I said. "You look good in diamonds." Her face suddenly brightened with a glow like a halogen lamp. I'll never forget her expression that day.

I still see her so clearly: that face, those lips, that nose, shot through by a twin pair of nostrils. And especially those eyes. What most people don't realize is that the color wasn't pure violet. It was a trick of light; her eyes held an amalgam of more subtle tinctures—mauve, onyx, fuchsia, indigo, and perhaps even a hint of sawgrass.

I dearly loved her, but toward the end I could tell she was becoming too dependent on me. She tried to hide the fact by withdrawing—by growing critical. My height enables me to carry a few extra pounds, but she considered four hundred too many.

"You're getting fat," she remarked one night in the early '70s, while we were watching news coverage of Watergate.

"Fat?" I said indignantly. "You mean me?"

"Yes, you! You look like a camel lying there—*and* eating another éclair!"

"What about you?" I shot back. "You drift in here like the Hindenburg and accuse *me* of being fat?"

That set her off, and we had another quarrel. Yes, believe it or not, Elizabeth Taylor could get into quarrelsome moods—but I always believed we were meant to be together. Her tantrums and insults were a classic defense mechanism. It was her way of telling me that she adored me—and always would.

It's wonderful knowledge to have in my heart.

David Ferrell

According to Nostradamus, It's Really All About Me

For five hundred years, Nostradamus has remained a fascinating and polarizing figure—revered by some, ridiculed by a huge number of real idiots with nothing better to do. Believers claim that the enigmatic French seer, who died in 1566, foretold the great upheavals of the modern age: plagues, wars, and the rise and fall of Nazi Germany. Skeptics assert that an infinite number of monkeys, typing at even a modest forty words per minute, would eventually produce phrases like, "Hitler invades France," and, "Hitler is the fucking antichrist, nan-nee nan-nee nan-neeee!"

Blue-nosed cynics correctly observe that Nostradamus failed to predict many of the most basic aspects of modern life, including laptop computers, television streaming services, and drive-thru burger joints. Similar arguments are advanced by white-nosed, green-nosed, and brown-nosed cynics as well; some even add to the list by saying Nostradamus didn't predict washing machines either, or the James Webb Space Telescope.

Like he had time!

Ascertaining the true magnitude of the prophet's psychic gifts is particularly challenging because, in the bleak and violent 1500s, fortune-tellers were regarded as heretics and often burned at the stake or executed on the guillotine. Typical of many otherwise gallant men (and women) of his time, Nostradamus was averse to being set on fire, and he especially opposed the idea of having his head chopped off. The common recourse was to avoid, at all costs,

Insults May Vary

the frightening possibility of being branded a "soothsayer." For Nostradamus, that meant deliberately disguising his prophecies as poetry—stanzas he labeled *quatrains*. He further protected himself by publishing the predictions under fanciful pseudonyms like "Walt Whitman," "e.e. cummings," and "William Shakespeare."

Scholars today give serious study only to the hundreds of verses directly attributed to Nostradamus himself. It is widely acknowledged that many of these convoluted writings—encoded with anagrams, hashtags, squiggly lines, and arrows—can be understood properly only if sung by a rapper ingesting psilocybin mushrooms.

It is of little surprise, then, that extensive portions of the seer's *oeuvre* still await successful interpretation.

Fortunately for all, I am able to fill in huge gaps in the historical record by offering this simple truth: in stanza after stanza, Nostradamus gazes toward the impossibly distant future and writes about a man of our present era who, while clearly important and presumably destined for greatness—why else would Nostradamus single him out?—remains at this moment unknown to the world at large.

Who is this mystery man?

Me.

Consider this early quatrain:

The great Empire will soon be exchanged
for a small place, which soon will begin to grow.
A small place of tiny area in the middle of which
he will come to lay down his scepter.

Here, Nostradamus, in a chilling blaze of insight, zeroes in on the repercussions of my first divorce, when Mary Ann destroyed me both emotionally and financially. Her cold-hearted aggression forced us to give up our spacious neo-colonial manse (the "great Empire") and relocate—in my case, into a claustrophobic one-bedroom apartment ("a small place"). This snippet alone, so representative of the great prophet's writing, causes me to quiver with gooseflesh, so perfectly does it reflect my downward spiral at the time. A tiny hellhole "which will begin to grow"—not literally, of course, for the seer is alluding instead to the stubborn black mold that came to engulf much of the shower floor and the ceiling corners above it. My God, was it an awful problem.

Then, with characteristic brilliance, Nostradamus zeroes in on the worst moment of the breakup with the sly but meaningful phrase, "he will come to lay down his scepter." This bit of sexual symbolism is obvious to any twelve-year-old. It is a clear reference to Mary Ann's only visit to my apartment, to deal with a dispute over her credit cards. Sad to say, the conflict escalated, and she showed the indelicate, rotten judgment to plant a knee in my groin. I was immediately obliged to lay down my scepter—along with the accompanying pair of crown jewels. In fact, my entire body was on the floor while she stalked out like a wooden soldier.

Dark times.

Here's another well-known stanza:

Beasts ferocious from hunger will swim across rivers:
The greater part of the region will be against the Hister,
The great one will cause it to be dragged in an iron cage,
When the German child will observe nothing.

Scholars are nearly unanimous that this riveting quatrain identifies the Nazi blitzkrieg and, but for a minor misspelling, even cites Adolf Hitler by name.
Incredible!
But wrong.

Insults May Vary

In actuality, Nostradamus is writing about my Thanksgiving dinner in 2017, a year after I'd settled into a new rental house in San Diego. "Beasts ferocious from hunger" perfectly describes the horde of family, in-laws, and friends who descended into my well-ordered world, screwing it up for five long hours. Just as the great mystic wrote, two of the monsters—my young twin nephews, Dwight and Duane—would swim across nearby Lennart Creek within scant months of the feast.

Hister? With all due respect to the eggheads and dingbats who continue to obsess over World War II, Nostradamus was not referring to Hitler; he meant (missing by only a single letter!) my sister Cynthia, who, shortly before the pecan pie, tried to float the notion that electric cars and rooftop solar panels should be mandatory in the U.S. Her suggestion was immediately shot down by "the greater part" of the gathering; i.e., just about everyone at the table.

The "iron cage" can only mean my antique stove (an avocado-green O'Keefe and Merritt), where, of course, I dragged out the turkey—slightly charred on top but quite edible. And as to the "German child," whom Nostradamus said would observe nothing, I could go on and on about my German neighbor up the street, Hilda. A girl only in the metaphorical sense—she was a giggly, straw-haired legal secretary of thirty-seven who insinuated herself into my life the way certain predatory species take over the nest of another: looking like they belong, but meanwhile, they devour the eggs.

Hilda exploited my unwarranted kindness and generosity for the better part of eight months before the tantrums started (mostly mine), exacerbated by her trysts with three other men—two of whom, I believe, were half-brothers, and one who I know for a fact organized rooster fights in El Cajon. And somehow, out of the mess, Hilda was able to prevail upon her boss—one of those soulless, brass-knuckle lawyers you read about—to obtain a restraining order against me.

Observe nothing? She was not invited! Of course she observed nothing!

Let's move on.

Consider this remarkable prognostication:

In the conflict the great one who was worth little
At his end will perform a marvelous deed:
While 'Adria' will see what he was lacking,
During the banquet the proud one stabbed.

An uncanny summation of my second divorce! This was about Adela, the harping one. The seer nearly nails the spelling—"Adria"—and locks onto her assessment of my self-esteem, which truly must have been lacking because, really, why would I have married her?

The line *At his end will perform a marvelous deed* specifically references the final days of our union, which, I'll tell you, came none too soon—and coincided with the end of my sanity. It was ego death and the death of my soul, all wrapped into one. I do wonder what *marvelous deed* the seer was specifying, because frankly, I performed an abundance of them.

Finally, the most dramatic line of the quatrain—about a *"banquet"* and the *"proud one"* being stabbed—must be another metaphorical reference to what I endured after renting a single-wide trailer near the Bekins warehouse. For a long while, I lived on Banquet brand frozen dinners. I maintained my pride, however, and rarely accepted handouts, despite her having bled me dry. *Stabbed?* You bet. Adela spent years stabbing me in the back with scurrilous attacks on my reputation. It's what she does.

The amazing Nostradamus did not limit himself to my domestic woes. Look at this one:

Insults May Vary

He who has overcome the hazards,
Who has ne'er dreaded sword, fire, water,
And of the country very close to Toulouse,
By a blow of steel the entire world astonished,
Strangely given by the Crocodile,
People delighted to see such a spectacle.

I chuckled to read such a clear summation of my golfing trip to Florida in 2022—sand traps, water hazards and all. The key element of the quatrain is the splendid eagle I scored at a course in Miami, when, after landing in a dozen straight bunkers, I whacked a titanic slice with a three-iron (*"a blow of steel"*) that skirted a manicured lake occupied by one of the Sunshine State's federally protected reptiles.

Astounded guests at the umbrella tables outside the clubhouse burst into applause as my ball rolled lickety-split into the cup. I thrust a fist to the sky and spotted Tiger himself (it looked like him, anyway) holding an iced tea and laughing.

These and other examples are so compelling that I have to wonder if Nostradamus was some sort of psychic stalker, tracking my every movement from across the reaches of time.

Which leads to questions about what still lies ahead. Although the great prophet's manuscripts are notoriously difficult to interpret, I feel certain, after thousands of hours of careful study, that my destiny is richly embroidered with giddy triumphs and—why is Fate so cruel?—a ceaseless succession of the same sorts of godawful disasters that have plagued my life so far.

To be more specific, the quatrains suggest that I am to inherit the vast wine-cork collection of a painfully thin New York stage dancer who will die swimming the English Channel in 2036. It seems clear that I will be abducted from a street corner in New Haven, Conn., and tarred and feathered by drunken college frat brothers who mistake me for someone else. After a thug attacks me with a crowbar in Los Angeles, shattering my kneecap, I will win either a boat or a booby prize on a television game show.

When the moon is in Sagittarius, in 2038, I will spot a dollar bill under a parked car and wrench my back trying to retrieve it. A few years later, when *"the comet runs in Aquarius,"* I will trip on a half-empty Coke can and tumble down a marble stairway, breaking my elbow and knocking out my right eye tooth. A redhead will break my heart, then a blonde, and in my final years, when *"the great cycle completes in Taurus,"* I'll cohabitate near an industrial plant with two parakeets and an illegally kept spider monkey.

My death will *"occur without sorrow,"* Nostradamus writes, and will be mercifully quick. No long period of suffering for me: *"The deed to be done by a fiery thunderbolt from the heavens,"* which, considering the context, could mean a jet crash, a meteor, or a rocket-propelled explosive device.

A Genius at Work in Real Time

It's rare for the MacArthur Foundation, bestower of the coveted "Genius Grants," to name a finalist who has yet to achieve a high degree of creative success. Writer Frank van Slyke is a stunning exception, having made this year's short list despite a track record that one insider bluntly dismissed as "abysmal." The fact that Frank remains unpublished at age thirty-six proved less important to senior members of the screening committee than his "unequaled passion" for his work; Frank was hailed as "a creative juggernaut," based in large part on his prolific output of more than eight thousand essays, poems, short stories, and novels—all kept in boxes in his apartment.

In an unusual component of the review, Frank was asked to submit a real-time chronicle of his daily writing process. He dictated the following on a chilly March morning in New York City:

Facing the keyboard, just as Hemingway once did, just as legions of transcendent writers have done down through the years, and, in fact, as the very best of them continue to do today, I reflect on the magnitude of the task before me—writing. Am I up to it, having had my full night's sleep? Am I ready?

Yes!

My focus is laser-like; now is the time. My coffee is here. By now I've had five cups, and my nervous system is singing like a high-voltage wire. I settle into my battered old writing chair—my trusty chair—and take another sip. Several more sips, all the while gazing, exactly as Steinbeck must have done, at the keys arrayed before me. Staring at them the same way Ring Lardner and Edith Wharton stared, and Kurt Vonnegut and Raymond Chandler and Sam Shepard, too. Eyes fixed on those keys. The "Z" and "X" on the lower left, obediently waiting, and the curious "?" key on the bottom right, adjoining that long key marked "shift." All of them ready for me.

Given the gravity of my thoughts, the grand themes I hope to address—no, no, *aspire* to address—I wish for more keys. More letters. There should be thousands of letters to help wring every last nuance of meaning out of this whirling, madcap world, our wild and truculent existence. It's actually a shock that Hemingway could suffice with the existing bare-bones alphabet. Surely his prose would have exhibited an extra dimension of suppleness and style if there were, say, thirty letters. Or thirty-five.

I'd invent a few new ones to occupy a space between "K" and "L," I think, and maybe between "R" and "S" as well. Or at the end, after "Z." I'd add several really squiggly letters and a comparable number with straight lines and clean angles. Maybe something horizontal, like an equal sign with a tiny curlicue between the dash lines. Not to digress too far here, but I've made quite a few suggestions in writing—in dozens of pieces of correspondence—arguing for a "triple-U" and a box-shaped letter that would be called a "square" (or "capital square"), or, if not that, a "doyette" (and "capital doyette"), which I cannot even begin to describe but would be a very, *very* cool-looking letter, believe me.

Those letters—the correspondence, I mean—are in stamped envelopes, ready to go once I figure out where to send them.

Needless to say, I've wondered many times—and perhaps you have, too—about Shirley Hazzard: To what extraordinary literary heights might she have soared if only she had possessed an adequate number of letters to accommodate her exceptional mind? Ditto for Saul Bellow. What the guy might have done with even *one more vowel*—just a single vowel, for god's sake!

Insults May Vary

Not that it matters now. The hourglass drains. Hazzard, Bellow, and their peers have gone, and I have raised aloft the torch, carrying on the journey. The letters of the keyboard, a paltry lot to be sure, await the urging of my fingers. I stare hard and think about each key in turn. It's my destiny, it seems, to begin pressing them. But which ones?

I lurch to my feet and move to the window. A blur of movement, up and across the room to the window, jauntily pirouetting on the way. I hold fiercely to the belief that freedom is an essential element of writing: the freedom to express any thought, any action. The freedom to go and look out the window—and to pirouette on the way, if I so choose. Hell, I could even leap out the fucking window, if it comes to that, though so far, thankfully, I haven't gone that far. Not at all. I'm not crazy. Don't forget, I live on the seventh floor— I would die!

For long moments, I stare down into the frenetic street below. Proust must have done this in his time. Fitzgerald, too. Step away to marshal thoughts. Maybe stare out the window for a bit.

Cars go by, and a teenager down below is talking to a girl. No, he's actually talking on a cell phone, and the girl just happens to be standing near him. Christ, you little shit, *talk to her!* She's right there!

Idiot! The girl is right there! She's definitely cute!

Pressing keys is not a winning plan, I realize. Mere pressing is too indifferent, passive, inadequate—like firing a slingshot when you need a good shotgun blast. With the power of my ideas, my intellect as deep as an ocean trench, pent-up emotion seething in the fiery furnace of my tortured soul, I need to do more than merely press.

Emboldened, I stride back to my chair and drop into it like a great fluttering bird, like a falcon swooping down, or Poe's raven careening down from the bust of Pallas and alighting on a familiar perch: my worn and beaten old swivel chair. I assume the classic writing position and once again let my eyes fall on the neat constellation of keys. My mind revving up, no doubt advancing from alpha waves to beta and on into delta and theta and God knows what else—even as wondrous themes flash through my frontal lobe like fork lightning. This is the best me, the ethereal me, the gathering storm fomenting a maelstrom of neural activity, fantastic insights galore. My fingers grope forward and I *pound*—not press—*pound* on the keys.

I wokke up in mmy pajkamas and ;my thraot qwas dry.

Stopping to regard this brief creative flurry, I recognize (who wouldn't?) several typographical errors. These I fix immediately—why wait?—and then I smile at seeing the clear literary merits of the opening of my story. It's a bold and declarative sentence, as honest and unflinching as Hemingway might have written, *if* he had slept with his mouth open.

The blood of the kill is now in my nostrils, so to speak. Metaphor alert: If the goal is to find the ever-elusive story line, if that is the prey, then call me the hunter, the wolf on the prowl. Like Thomas Wolfe. Or Tom Wolfe. Virginia Woolf. The whole pack of us. Wolves of the keyboard. *The strength of the pack is the wolf.* That's me. Kipling wrote that. He was another, pounding on the keys. Like I do.

Sensing a direction, filled now with a lust for verbs and predicates, I concentrate my mind, just as Dickens and Tolstoy did so often. Like Jane Austen. Mark Twain. With Twain-like gravitas, I hunch forward, trying to conceive a second sentence. My fingers begin flying and, with that ineluctable magic that owes chiefly to the Muses, a result appears.

I reached for my glass of water on the nightstand.

Again correcting trifling errors, I feel a thrill dampened only by a looming puzzle: *What next?* The aim is scintillating fiction, not some banal retelling of a lousy moment waking up. What becomes of the fictional me at this vulnerable moment of paralyzing dry-mouth? Do I quench my thirst? Or clumsily knock the glass onto the floor, spilling the water on the carpet, bringing about (in a later

Insults May Vary

chapter) smelly mildew?

Perhaps the glass is empty. If so, do I shuffle sullenly into the kitchen? Or spew a stream of noisy curses?

Rising in thought, I pace the floor, aware that my narrative has reached a critical turning point. Already. I gaze out the window. The same guy is still in the street, still yakking on the cell. The girl is gone.

Oh my God, what symbolism! I grab an index card and headline it, *Note to self.* "There was a girl on the sidewalk," I write. "Now she's gone!"

Jesus Christ, that's powerful. That says it all. The intensity of it engulfs me. I feel a need to leave the room—at least for a while. Hemingway would have recognized the same deep need in himself. He would have gone out and shot a lion or hauled in a marlin, cooked it over an open flame, and eaten the firm and meaty flesh with his bare hands. Then he would have wandered into town and seen Paco, the blind boy, and spoken to him in broken Spanish. Their words would have saddened him and heartened him and made him laugh. He would have stopped for a drink and to see Clara, who had been on the road in Algiers, and who was troubled, though she wouldn't say why—not at first.

Hemingway would have got the truth out of her, eventually.

But he's Hemingway. I'm different. I wander into the kitchen instead and eat a peanut butter cookie. I brush away the crumbs and return to the keyboard.

With a couple of key clicks, I delete most of the story and start over.

I woke up in my pajamas and reached for the TV remote.

Yeah, that's nice. A better start. Simple and direct. Relatable. That's the life—lying around in your PJs and watching TV.

I wonder what's on right now.

Maybe I'll write tomorrow.

David Ferrell

Tour Notes of a Spoken Word Artist

With his remarkable—dare I proclaim it *glorious*?—maturation, Ross Michael Rayburn has burst forth from the chrysalis of his exceptional early promise to become the greatest spoken word artist alive today, bar none. Every syllable, so exquisitely rendered, so rich in timbre, demonstrates that he has eclipsed Rubinstein, Gomez, and Beckwith, and stands as perhaps the only modern equal of 18th-century powerhouse Wilma Montagne.

At only twenty-six, Rayburn's triumphs include the release of his ninth album, *Symphony of the Larynx*, and a subsequent twelve-week, fourteen-city tour that can only be labeled stupendous. Few would dispute that his intellectually bracing, one-word "spoken concerts" mark a watershed advancement of American culture. Scalpers are commanding $12,000 a seat—extraordinary, considering that Rayburn's performances rarely last longer than ten to fifteen seconds, including his much-lauded dramatic pauses.

Fortunately, a film crew shot extensive footage of the recent tour for a forthcoming Ken Burns documentary series. Even more important, historically, may be the personal journals that Rayburn has kept since childhood. Excerpts reveal a sensitive superstar who somehow shines despite near-crippling insecurity and self-doubt.

4/9 — Minneapolis.
So much excitement. The Target Center! Huge crowd for kick-off night. Spent hours beforehand with H and T, agonizing over

final choice for the word. By then we had narrowed it down to six possibilities. H pushed for *kaboom*—direct, emphatic, full of impact. T insisted on more syllables: *lullaby*. Soothing and rhythmic. A sexier word, I had to agree. *Lullaby*. Could I pull off the *L* sound? On opening night?! Jitters beyond belief. No decision by final sound check, nor by "go" time. Mounted the steps to the high podium wondering, *Can I do this?* Vast sea of faces out there in the semi-darkness. Crackling tension. An engulfing silence. My throat dry as old shoe leather. Sipped my water, aware of the thudding of my heart. Fast and drum-like. So afraid of my voice quavering—which only heightened the possibility! Finally threw caution to the wind and went off script. "*Goldfish*," I said, drawing it out. *Gollld-fisssshh*. Hit hard on the sibilance, filling the place with snake-like *S* sounds. Pandemonium! Cheers and more cheers! People standing, shouting. Love the people of Minneapolis. So warm, such a highly intelligent crowd. Raucous celebrating afterward. T was fine about the surprise switcheroo, totally out of left field. It worked out, she said. H seemed miffed. Really wanted *kaboom*. Eventually he came around, though. Very late night. Cocktails, cocktails. Oh my, what a start!

4/16 — St. Louis.

Noun or verb tonight? My instinct was to mix it up, go for a strong, even wacky, action verb. H pushed hard again for *kaboom*. For some reason I bristled, resenting the pressure, and we ended up quarreling. I'm not sure why—I'd prefer saving *kaboom* for Kansas City or Detroit. Or Indianapolis. Just a gut feeling. T ran through a long list of verbs. Nothing seemed exactly right. We settled on *excavate*. Many second thoughts, but I was won over by the notion of multi-syllables. Give the crowd a little extra. A compound word they wouldn't hear every day. Still, I felt unease, a sense of wrongness. Why? An hour before curtain, I called H and T to my dressing room and announced a peremptory change: it would be *lullaby*.

"*Lullaby? Lullaby is not a verb,*" H said, in that tone of his that I hate. The brittle, accusatory tone that masks so much of his own self-loathing. T, of course, was overjoyed. *Lullaby is so seductive,* she declared. Loved the way she said *seductive*. Lots of energy in the building, again. Harsh spotlights, nerves, but the L sounds proved no challenge. The entire word flowed out like honey. T was right. Everyone went nuts! Went crazy. God, I love hearing that adoration! Am I mad? Who cares? I gloried in it. Couldn't sleep until nearly dawn.

4/20 — Kansas City.

Sat in a funky '50s diner, anguishing as always over my options. Noticed a word on the menu that struck my fancy: *bacon-burger.* My God, the alliteration! H voiced tepid support, looking to regain my good graces, but I could see in his flinty little eyes that he was still thinking *kaboom*. It was all but written on his forehead, the bastard. T pointed out a dessert selection: *meringue*. Worth considering. I couldn't rule it out. *Meringue.* We've got to know by tomorrow night.

4/21 — Kansas City.

Local reporter gave me a big write-up in today's *Star*, as if I needed more attention. Madhouse at the arena. Cameras flashing, rabid people pushing through the aisles. I got up there, staring out over that adoring throng, and hit them with a doozy—*doozy*. You'd have thought Jesus was on stage with the Beatles! My poor eardrums! I have to pinch myself sometimes, I really do.

4/28 — Detroit.

Is it possible to sustain it, this incredible momentum? So many amazing highs and yet the pressure is always on. I feel an intense need to equal or surpass every previous performance. Prowled the lakefront, running scores of words through my head—maybe hundreds—until it occurred to me to think of these concerts in *toto*, as a series of discrete but somehow unified experiences. A jolting thought: Am I falling short, failing in some profound way, because I lack an overarching theme? Sudden, crippling anxiety. The whole afternoon in bed, my mind racing. A theme? When I couldn't even tell you tomorrow night's plan?

4/29 — Detroit.

"What's the word?" H said very directly, hoping, of course, that I would announce at long last that it would be *kaboom*. He didn't have to say so—I could read the little fucker's mind. *Kaboom* was stuck in there like a dragonfly in amber. I didn't say so, but I wouldn't do *kaboom* now if it was the only word in the dictionary. Glancing up from my latte—we were in the Marriott lobby—I broached the idea of a grand theme. He looked incredulous, and so did T, actually. *This far into the tour?*

I noted the huge opening-night success with *goldfish*. "Maybe fish in general. Or sea creatures writ large. I could see doing *walrus*."

H looked stricken. "We're on a roll, and you want to change it? Part of the thrill's the uncertainty. You want to narrow your range to fish?"

We argued about it. I both pitied him and hated him. No, I *loathed* him. All my life, skeptics and doubters have fueled me. Right then and there I resolved to exploit a whole ocean of aquatic terms. Algae to zebrafish. The little prick will wait till doomsday before he hears *kaboom*.

4/29 — Detroit.

Stepped right out into the spotlight and gave it to them: *dorsal fin*. A huge response. Tremendous ovation. T grinned from ear to ear. H tried to look happy for me, mostly in vain. I'm sick of his resentments. He'll be gone when this tour is done.

5/6 — Indianapolis.

T smiled at me during sound check; she looked lovely—pixie hair, faded jeans. I realized how in-sync we are; we just click. Something good might be happening. Just let it unfold. Happy, happy. Another enormous crowd, electricity in the building. Stood poised at the mic a long time, aware of the cameras, the deepening hush. Everyone waiting. Then I came at them with a subtle nasal twang: *narwhal*. Really drew out the *aarrrr* sound, kept the *L* crisp and "wet," like an arctic bay. Huge applause. Very nice applause—despite seeing a few puzzled faces. Clearly, there needs to be more public awareness of narwhals. They're an underappreciated species.

5/14 — Des Moines.

Finally went with *walrus*. Huge winner! Spectacular audience reaction. Love the people, I really do. Everyone adores a walrus, that's for sure. T had tipped off *The New Yorker*, which ran a short online piece about my "aquatic deep dive." Clever. Smiled and re-read the article twice. Wait 'til I do *starfish*.

5/23 — Shreveport.

Shock and heartbreak. Around 2 a.m. I cracked open the door of my penthouse suite, merely to set my empty plate of Crab Louie in the hallway for room service. Happened to see H emerging from T's suite. At 2 in the morning! He never looked my way, just slunk off toward the elevators like a scurrying little rat. A sneaky fuckhead rat.

I froze, blood turning to ice. Ice at first, and then melting slush. Half-frozen slushy blood bringing tremendous pain to my heart. I can't describe—really, I wanted to fire them both, fire H for sure. And T—how could she? God, I wanted to make a scene. Such key people in running the tour. To fire them might wreck everything. I needed to think.

Ignored them the next day. Cold shoulder treatment on steroids. Barely saw the big crowd. Went out there and ditched the plan—which was *moray eel*—and instead landed *treachery*. Big winner, actually. Gargantuan ovation. Looked right at T the whole time. She knew right away that I knew.

Went straight to my suite afterward, skipping the after party, and partook of the reefer.

5/28 — New Orleans.

Couldn't take another moment of H's presence. Fired his ass right in the men's room of the Biltmore. Ran into him in there and did the deed. *You're gone, mister. Kaboom!* Felt good to do it. Made me regular, believe it or not. Renewed, recharged, reinvigorated.

Skipped the prep meeting with T—might have been awkward. Just went on cold. Pure instinct. Long pause, drama, cameras rolling, shutters clicking, clicking, clicking, and I gave it to them: *urchin*. Cold, wet-sounding tone. *Urchin*. Nailed it big-time. Could still hear rippling cheers even as I ducked into the limo. Laughed like a maniac.

6/3 — Houston.

T quit. The bitch. Sent a vague text and I never saw her again. Crazy, ungrateful bitch—and of course I was devastated. Who wouldn't be? Scrambled for hours even with R taking over. Thankfully R's a decent chap. Nice word, *chap*. Short and crisp. He worked like a madman and we brought the curtain up on time. Audience never the wiser.

Kept my voice from cracking and delivered an emphatic *blowfish*. Loved the next morning's headline in the *Chronicle*: "*'Blowfish'—Rayburn Blows Away Packed Crowd.*"

6/9 — Dallas.

The trades got wind of it. *Spoken Word Review* ran a two-column news brief: H and T "tying the knot" after abandoning Rayburn tour. *Silver Tongue* mentioned a possible honeymoon in Barbados. Christ, what humiliation! Super tough day. Canceled interviews, took stage with an aching in my heart—and my throat.

It took all I had, but I managed to come out of the blue with a zinger: *perfidious*.

Hope they saw the news coverage. Hope they heard the crowd going nuts for me.

6/11 — Austin.

The limo struck an old lady's wheelchair just outside the arena. I wasn't in the mood for any more hassles. I saw her topple over and fought an urge to yell out the window, *"Cross with the WALK sign! You're in the street!"* Felt sorry for her, though, and ordered the driver to stop, even though we were due at make-up.

It was a mess for half an hour. Luckily, they got the bleeding stopped with a big, turban-like bandage, and she looked very much alive when they whisked her away, siren blaring.

Not the best omen on another sold-out night. Felt oddly rattled as I climbed to the high stage. Took a couple of very deep breaths and managed to send the huge audience into delirium: *pompano*.

6/14 — San Antonio.

I suppose I'm not the first person to feel snakebit in Texas. More problems. This time a heckler showed up, a lunatic hollering from the orchestra pit: *"Lady killer! Lady killer!"*

At first I was flattered—what man wouldn't be?—but he grew so belligerent that security hauled him out. I paused at the mic, allowing the commotion to die down.

It was my night to do *octopus*. I'd been practicing "O" sounds all day—short "O" and long "O"—trying to get the contrast right. I wanted absolute silence. It took a while, but finally the arena got deathly quiet, and then the most scary, horrific thing happened: a massive ceiling speaker, dangling down big as a washing machine, let go somehow and came crashing to the stage.

Landed like a bomb five feet from me! Surely would have crushed me like a cockroach if R hadn't moved the lectern for a better filming angle. God almighty, about the loudest noise I had ever heard.

Thankfully I kept my wits. Crowd seemed absolutely stunned. I stood stock still, waiting for the murmurs to die down. Waiting for the arena goons to get the fallen speaker out of the way. They were running around like maniacs.

Meanwhile, the people were waiting for me. They wanted—almost demanded—that the show go on. I could see it in their faces. Every face was on me, and I did my part. Did it with gusto. Crowd exploded into cheers when I gave them the big one I'd been saving: *Ka-BOOM!*

David Ferrell

Strange Coincidences: Eight Billion People on Earth, and YOU Are the One Reading This!

Nearly everyone knows a story like that of Donald Neville, a potato wholesaler from Twin Falls, Idaho, who became shipwrecked while touring the Caribbean. The hapless Neville drifted for twenty-nine days in a rubber raft, surviving on rainwater and four cans of Pringles. Too weak to row and still miles from land, Neville came upon an abandoned motorboat containing a Thermos of hot coffee as well as a Visa card and a photo ID of a different Donald Neville, a dog trainer from Delray Beach, Florida. The whereabouts of this second Donald Neville was, at the time, unknown and, in fact, continues to be a mystery.

Authorities say this other, missing Donald Neville most likely fell overboard and drowned; an alternative theory suggests he was murdered by his ex-wife, who was arrested three weeks later on unrelated arson charges after torching a bank teller's Ford Mustang. It is thought that the ex-wife may have disposed of her dead ex-husband's body in the Everglades and set the boat adrift without realizing there was a credit card and a Thermos still inside it. (A third scenario presents the possibility that one Donald Neville killed the other and that one or both men were using phony names for reasons unclear—possibly because they liked the name or because they belonged to some secret society of men using the alias Donald Neville—a clandestine organization whose membership, for all we know, might number in the hundreds or even the thousands. If the latter is the case, it's safe to say that the threads of deception might be so elaborate and intricately entwined that no one will ever untangle the mess—and the murder, if that's what it was, surely must rank as one of the most clever and diabolical crimes ever committed!)

But let's not digress. What is definitively known is that the Twin Falls Donald Neville—the first one I mentioned—very closely resembled the Delray Beach Donald Neville, with the same wispy, reddish hair and long, pointy beard, enabling the Twin Falls Don Neville to motor right into port at Saint Kitts and, after recuperating a bit, eat, drink, and dance the night away for seven weeks, until the Visa was maxed out.

Imagine the odds that one Donald Neville would find a Visa card belonging to another Donald Neville—in the middle of the ocean!—and that the two men would look like brothers. And that a potato man with no prior criminal record would be sufficiently bold as to skip a light fandango with another poor bastard's credit card to the tune of a seven-week spending spree!

Remarkable events such as this occur far more frequently than we might realize. They are a compelling sign of the deep causal interconnectedness of the universe—the fact that some higher intelligence—God or "the godhead" or "Jehovah" or (alternatively) "Yehovah" or (alternatively to that) "Yehowah"—is up there screwing with us, orchestrating bizarre events as if to yuk it up at our expense, although who knows what the real purpose is?

Surely it's blasphemous to accuse the Big Guy of putting a lit match to the toes of pitiable humans struggling to get by on a hostile planet. Certainly, there is always a higher purpose, isn't there? A purpose that's always a part of a larger master plan?

Ponder that while perusing these three additional examples of amazing coincidences, compiled from the files of *Coincidental Happenstance* magazine:

Case No. 1:

On Nov. 21, a lumberjack in northern Oregon was scaling the trunk of a Douglas fir without wearing the mandatory safety harness. Thirty feet up, he was startled by a squirrel darting toward him in an "almost aggressive way," causing him to lose his balance and fall; he broke his right wrist and forearm and dislocated his shoulder. That hapless lumberjack's name was Larry R. Blanchard. According to information later gleaned from social media posts and a very, very talented remote viewer, Blanchard was wearing blue jeans, a red plaid Pendleton shirt, and a pair of Hanes white all-cotton men's briefs. As he dropped like a flailing scarecrow, he was heard to scream or shriek something like, "Aaaaaa-AAAAAAh!"

On exactly the same day, a high school teacher in Fort Lauderdale, Fla., named Ruben R. Torres (the same middle initial!) was on a ladder hanging Christmas lights from the eaves of his garage when he, too, lost his balance and fell, landing on his concrete driveway like a sack of cement. He, too, broke his wrist (albeit the left one) and dislocated his shoulder. According to the teacher's wife, who kept telling him to watch out, be careful, don't lean so far out, the teacher—like the lumberjack—cried out "Aaaaaaaah!" or possibly "Aaaaarrr-RRRAAAAHHH!" on the way down. Torres, like Blanchard, wore Hanes all-cotton briefs, but not the white ones—a gray pair. Both men owned a car, and both men had recently eaten a hamburger accompanied by a diet drink. The similarities do not stop there, no sirree. Each of these reckless victims of Earth's gravitational field had taken a compulsory science class in high school, and each was behind on paying his electric bill. Each had seen the previous year's Super Bowl, and each had blown money playing the slots in Las Vegas.

Incredibly, neither man knew the other; no, let's not assume the veracity of such a claim. It's more accurate to say that—with no apparent prior communication—each man denied knowing the other. They flatly denied it.

Case No. 2:

At first blush, no two people could have seemed more different. Esther Laughlin was a fifty-eight-year-old mortgage appraiser who

Insults May Vary

lived near Nob Hill in San Francisco. She was finicky, white-haired, clinically obese (despite a succession of low-carb diets), and she loved the opera (especially Pavarotti) nearly as much as she loved chili fries and tiramisu. Don Gwynn was a twenty-two-year-old skateboard pro from Los Angeles. He wore spiked black hair (a frightening look) and a shiny steel ring in his nose. He was as skinny as one of the stairway rails he liked to careen down at risk to life and limb.

Like the two men cited in Case No. 1, these individuals lived far apart and moved within vastly different social spheres. It's all but certain that Laughlin and Gwynn had never met, nor had they planned on meeting—each was, apparently, wholly unaware of the other. Yet in 2018, they were both in San Francisco at the same time! In fact, on May 9 of that year, in a stunning case of temporary parallel lives (TPL)—a phenomenon explored at length in Simon Hagel's excellent book, *Coincidences Do Happen, Often at the Same Time!*—both the mortgage lender and the skateboard pro walked into the same airport, San Francisco International, at approximately the same time. Stranger still, they converged like a pair of homing pigeons—or, perhaps more aptly, like two lovers who had carefully schemed an illicit rendezvous—reaching the same gate and boarding the same jet flight to Los Angeles! Stranger than even that—and now we're talking laughably, almost impossibly strange—Laughlin and Gwynn sat in the same row (!), in two adjoining (!) seats (6D and 6E), and they did meet, against odds so astronomical that, believe me, you could never begin to comprehend.

Taking off at literally the same instant, these two disparate souls traveled on a perfectly parallel course (a defining feature of the TPL phenomenon) in a southbound direction (even as the offshore wind blew from the west) all the way to Los Angeles, where they disembarked from the plane but continued their extraordinary TPL dance. Laughlin stopped briefly in a restroom, and Gwynn also stopped briefly in a restroom. Afterward—though no longer speaking (not because of any grudge or "bad blood," but the plain

David Ferrell

fact is they were "beyond words" in some intuitive, mystical way)—well, believe it or not, these two travelers proceeded simultaneously down the same long corridor, exiting through the same broad doorway marked *TO GROUND TRANSPORTATION*.

No one knows whether they boarded identical cabs or Uber cars and drove on to the same restaurant, hotel, or nightclub, but Hagel, who gives this case its own compelling chapter, suggests it was virtually inevitable that somewhere, at a future point in time, their life paths would overlap again—even if only in some subtle way, such as gazing at the moon on the same night—because they had formed such a high degree of physical and psychical entanglement.

Stay tuned for updates.

Case No. 3:

The spookiest—and most nearly tragic—of these incredible stories involves a Lyft driver and a man specializing in heater and air-conditioning repair in suburban Denver, Colorado. Already, there is the specter of remarkable coincidence: they live in the same city. The case goes far deeper, however. On a spring day (spring for both of them!), they left their homes in the morning (within half an hour of each other) and began driving—both of them, despite the myriad other activities that either could have chosen, such as weeding the front lawn or playfully spinning along the sidewalk with arms outstretched, pretending to be a tornado or the Tasmanian Devil in one of the old Warner Bros. cartoons, perhaps while also emitting a high-pitched whirring noise as if rotating at thousands of RPMs.

Paul Dornheiser, in his ground-breaking book *Déjà Vu for Two*, points out that the Lyft driver, Leo Gannon, needed new front brakes for his Chevy, while the repairman, Dennis Lohaus, was overdue for an oil change—a clear instance of coincidental deferred maintenance (CDM). However, it should be noted that the two men were traveling in different directions. The Lyft driver, Gannon, headed generally east and then south toward downtown, eventually

Insults May Vary

descending a freeway ramp and following Colfax Boulevard eastbound again. The repairman, Lohaus, went the opposite way—west. He veered south for a bit, then headed west again, and made a sharp turn south, crossing Colfax (get this!) at exactly (!) the same time (!) that Gannon was going by!

Although it strains credibility to say, the Lyft car and the air-conditioning repair van actually collided (!!!) at one of the busy intersections, where both men—not one, but both!—exited their vehicles and approached one another, meeting for the first time ever, much as the opera fan and the skateboard pro did on the plane.

This encounter, though, lacked the pleasant conviviality of a plane ride; in fact, Gannon hauled off and slugged Lohaus in the face! Seconds later, in the final coincidental moment of the encounter, Lohaus slugged Gannon in the face!

Two men, at almost exactly the same time, slugging each other in the face!!!!!

We need not dwell on the aftermath—the minor fracas that ensued—for police ended it quickly and Gannon endured scarcely an hour's treatment in the emergency room. The greater reality is the extraordinary coincidence involved—the overlapping experiences of two men joined by a common destiny.

Even the most hardened cynic has to shake his (or her) head and say, *whoa*, perhaps there really is some grand cosmic scheme far too vast and intricate for human comprehension.

Consider the question: *What brought you here, to this page, to this book, at this particular moment in time?**

Was it a bomb going off in an abandoned building in a blighted warehouse district? Or dogs howling in the wee hours outside your apartment window? Or something far more subtle—the whisperings of an ethereal voice set against the faint background hum of the universe?

* **Please post your stories on the author's website, using only words with seven or fewer letters.**

David Ferrell

The Mating Dance of Lawyers

Mark B. Schachter, Esq.
Senior Defense Attorney
Scheer, Willoughby & Myers

Dear Mr. Schachter,

Having reviewed your email proposal of this past Tuesday, June 4, I am pleased and, in fact, flattered by your nonbinding offer of social engagement henceforth to be termed the DINNER DATE or simply THE DATE.

While my support for the concept is, in principle, highly enthusiastic, this does not entirely mitigate certain feelings that might best be characterized as guarded or wary. I must note that such outings are inherently unpredictable. Possible outcomes range from embarrassment, humiliation, and psychological trauma (let's hope not!) to far more blissful results—even the chance, however remote, of an "ongoing relationship," cohabitation, or, in the extreme case, marriage. Any one of these would involve its own complexities, uncertainties, and obligations.

You and I know how terribly wrong almost any human interaction can go without a proper framework of contractual expectations. Therefore, I would ask that you please spell out with greater specificity exactly what you have in mind for the DINNER DATE—i.e., how long will it last? Where do you intend to take me? Not only will such details inform my decision, but should I accept, they will enable me to address important ancillary questions—for example, what time I should be ready, whether I should wear flats or fancy heels with my Dior pearl necklace, and so on.

Let us also be mindful that we are employed by competing law firms. Such a potentially dicey circumstance requires your assurance, in writing, that the DINNER DATE is in no way intended to seek a competitive advantage for Scheer, Willoughby, nor is it part of any long-range scheme by Scheer, Willoughby to orchestrate a corporate takeover of Kleiner, Williams, Hendrick & Barfield.

Furthermore, please allow me to clarify two key points of your memorandum:

1. Waiver of claims: It is imperative that we agree—time committed to THE DATE, both during the course of the event itself as well as in preparation and in the immediate aftermath (e.g., driving home), shall at no point be charged against the account of either party by the other, regardless of whether THE DATE is ultimately deemed worthwhile or not.

2. The curious line in your memorandum, "solely for mutual enjoyment and gratification," should in no way be construed as a promise on my part to participate in sexual acts, including but not limited to: a peck on the cheek, so-called heavy petting, foreplay, "French" kissing, mutual masturbation, fellatio (*God forbid!*), or various unsavory and extreme types of male aggression known in the popular jargon as "hiding the salami," "monkey dunking," "pounding the duck," or "wild-ass sucky fucky."

Surely you know me better than that, Mark!

I look forward to your reply.

Warmly,

Tricia R. Gilroony

Senior General Counsel

Kleiner, Williams, Hendrick & Barfield

David Ferrell

Dear Tricia,

Your note filled me with excitement and, I admit, a touch of trepidation, since it forced me to give much deeper thought to the myriad possible particulars and outcomes of our proposed DINNER DATE.

First, let me assure you that under no circumstance would I be so crass as to propose a formalized obligation on your part to yield up pleasures of the flesh, which, if given, should be offered voluntarily—out of feelings of true love and/or passionate desires that flare up unbidden in the scorching heat of the moment.

Similarly, I would never be so uncouth as to suggest a venue where flats would be the ideal women's attire (although I fully respect a woman's prerogative to dress in whatever style she chooses). In other words—keep that Dior necklace handy!

As per your request, here are my preliminary plans for the evening in question. I hope that by sharing these details I do not strip the DINNER DATE of its air of surprise and spontaneity, but rather lend to it an additional measure of anticipation and, dare I say, enticement.

The DINNER DATE shall at all times meet or exceed the minimum normal expectations for a formal romantic encounter involving salaried professionals drawing federally taxable annual incomes of greater than $300,000 (three hundred thousand dollars) and less than $1 million (one million dollars) per annum.

On the designated night, transportation will be provided to you free of charge at 7 p.m., whisking you from your doorstep to La Traviscalla in Beverly Hills, where all standard cocktails, specialty drinks, appetizers, and entrées will be offered—again, at no cost to you. Wine is available up to and including the $104-a-bottle Chateau Margaux cabernet sauvignon.

At your discretion, the DINNER DATE will conclude with dessert and coffee at Walt's Nook or a more traditional cocktail nightcap at Bar Marmont. You will be delivered home during a two-hour window between 11 p.m. and 1 a.m.

Insults May Vary

Inasmuch as the excursion is likely to cost the OFFERING PARTY (me) upwards of $400—or possibly even twice that—while costing you, the RESPONDENT, absolutely zilch, I suggest we drop the phrase "peck on the cheek" from your list of precluded sexual acts. A kiss is about the least a gentleman might hope for given such generosity. But let's not quibble over details—surely the sensibilities of the moment should govern our actions.

Please reply. I very much look forward to a wonderful outing with you.

Yours (hopefully),

Mark

Dear Mark,

You are every bit the persuasive, insightful gentleman I imagined you to be during our encounters at the courthouse. Eloquence and practicality are a rare (and winning) combination, and I admit to being all but smitten—even while I see a number of remaining issues that must be resolved before I agree to accompany you on the DINNER DATE.

Sad to say, I simply cannot go to La Traviscalla. That venue has been a house of horrors for me on the two occasions I've made the mistake of dining there. Apparently, I did not learn my lesson from a bouillabaisse of tainted mussels two years ago, despite the near-death experience of having my stomach pumped. Only last January, I took my mother there to fête her 83rd birthday.

A rather slapstick mishap involving a pineapple rhubarb flambé badly scorched—permanently scarring—my poor mother's nose. (My firm is handling her lawsuit.) Only an icy-cold drenching administered by a quick-thinking man with a water pitcher kept the leaping flames from burning off every hair on her head.

Surely you can suggest an alternative that doesn't have such lousy acoustics, snooty waiters, and revolting décor.

Secondly, let's clarify this matter of the goodnight kiss. A literal reading of your note suggests you view a kiss as remittance to the man offsetting the cost of the date. Mark, I cannot tell you how offensive that attitude is! Obliging a woman to "put out" in exchange for cash favors presents a slippery slope whose logical end has her giving massages in the red-light district.

One night it's a kiss, soon enough a hand job. Before you know it, she's spread-eagle on her back while some drunken Lothario's distended member jackhammers toward her ovaries.

Surely, Mark, you dashed off your note under some duress and did not pause to consider the implicit ramifications of what you were saying. Perhaps your mind was clouded by the travails of some hapless (albeit probably guilty) defendant who entrusts you to save him from his rightful demise in the gas chamber. I am favorably inclined to forgive the affront—with a modest word or two of apology from you.

In fact, I urge us to settle these few matters and get on to the happier task of deciding on a night. In anticipation of your reply, I've asked my assistant to begin preparing a draft agreement, TERMS AND CONDITIONS OF THE DINNER DATE, spelling out these and numerous other, smaller details. I've attached a preliminary copy for your review.

Eagerly awaiting your next reply,
Tricia

Dear Tricia,

You are nothing if not thorough! I stayed up late last night reading all thirty-eight pages of TERMS AND CONDITIONS OF THE DINNER DATE. I gather that much of it is boilerplate, though I was taken aback by the stipulation on page 12, paragraph 9, subsection C) that I should not wear a blue shirt. It so happens that, of all the colors beyond basic white, blue is the one that looks especially good on me owing to the cast of my complexion.

Insults May Vary

In fact, I anticipated picking you up in my sky-blue Ralph Lauren dress shirt, cobalt-and-crimson striped tie, and my Brioni charcoal herringbone suit—a combination I wore to excellent effect on the day of the Magruder verdict (he was acquitted), and which, on a separate occasion, turned the head of no less a discerning woman than Sandra Bullock when I happened to walk past her on Sunset Boulevard.

Please strike that needless and annoying paragraph and subsection. Note that it is within my rights to wear barber-pole stripes if I so choose.

Now, the venue. If La Traviscalla is out, I would happily suggest Bumgardner's instead—a locale I should have offered in the first place. The prime rib is sensational, as are all the steaks and salads. Service is superb, and the woodsy, low-key milieu ideal for intimate conversation. Plus, the valet parking is free and soup or salad comes with every entrée, meaning I could go bigger on the wine—up to and including the $160-a-bottle Jordan pinot noir.

Finally, yes, I apologize for presuming that a well-entertained, grateful woman would want to end a romantic evening by giving her Prince Charming a peck on the cheek. Let's stipulate that there will be no goodnight kiss whatsoever (zero, none) unless you forcibly grab me by the lapels and pull me to your mouth for a full frontal face-lock. (I gather I have a greater chance of kissing Margot Robbie.)

Is that it? As you surmised, I am about to litigate a particularly complex case involving a heinous crime, and I would love to spend a wonderful evening in your company without having to devote every last waking hour to hashing out the terms of our DINNER DATE.

Please advise me as to where we stand and whether I need to sign the revised TERMS AND CONDITIONS ahead of time.

Mark

David Ferrell

Dear Mark,

Once again, you brought a smile to my lips with your latest missive. I dare say I felt a flutter in my heart when I pictured your tall, dashing form striding down Sunset Boulevard (bound for somewhere important, I bet!) in your cobalt tie and herringbone suit. I am only surprised that Sandra Bullock did not stop you and insist on having a drink together.

Please forgive me for the language in paragraph 9, subsection C) of page 12. As you noted, it is superfluous boilerplate and should have read: "the gentleman shall not wear a ROYAL blue [emphasis added], lime green, or magenta shirt, nor wear short sleeves," etc.

My assistant will revise the terms and conditions to that effect.

Mark, thank you for being so understanding concerning the goodnight kiss—strictly a matter of principle. I cannot foresee any awkwardness once we are together enjoying ourselves.

The only remaining point I'd like to address is the trifling question of "sweet nothings." It might seem silly to you (I dearly hope not), but the surest way to fry a woman's eggs is to have her go through the enormous trouble and anxiety of dressing up for a man—putting on, for instance, a stunning Cartier pendant and earrings and/or a knockout Donna Karan gown—only to have the stupid, inconsiderate dolt sit there the whole night gawking, without even once acknowledging how nice she looks.

I am confident that a true gentleman, which I believe you to be, would not object to a safeguard against such humiliation, and so I would ask for written assurance that you will direct at least three (3) sincere compliments my way during the course of the evening. One of these remarks might well be about the Dior necklace I mentioned earlier, should I decide to wear it, and if, in fact, you find it appealing.

I suggest that the remaining two compliments be of a "wildcard" nature that you can use however you see fit. As much as possible, these sweet nothings should catch me by surprise and be truly flattering.

Insults May Vary

It's not too much to ask, is it?
Thoughts?
Tricia

Dear Tricia,

Putting you at ease is certainly one of my top priorities—and, it so happens, a goal wholly compatible with the aims of our DINNER DATE.

I will gladly stipulate right now that your Dior pearl necklace is absolutely exquisite and looks especially fabulous on you, even though I have yet to actually lay eyes on it. If those superlatives are satisfactory, I will exclaim them with faux-spontaneous exuberance once we are settled into the unparalleled bliss of our night together.

As for sweet nothings two (2) and three (3), how much sincerity is required? God forbid—what if nothing else about your attire or demeanor cries out for a word of praise? Am I supposed to lie or make something up?

Just wondering.
Mark

Dear Mark,

You silly boy—though, of course, *boy* is strictly a colloquial term of affection, for you are a man both in chronological age and emotional maturity, as well as in every other relevant sense of the word. But back to the point: I would never (!) ask that you fabricate a compliment—not when there are so many obvious things about me (all modesty aside) that might invite a favorable comment from a man of your charms.

Let's suppose, hypothetically, that my necklace (wait until you see it!) is the only element of my attire that impresses you. You hate my dress, you hate my shoes, you hate the way I've done my hair.

Unlikely, but possible—and believe me, my keen woman's intuition will pick up that vibe if you're stewing in that sort of negativity. But OK, let's say you hate all these things—you might still find a way to praise my eyes or my smile.

Or you might play off a quip or humorous remark of mine—a laugh or chuckle followed by, "That was funny, Tricia," or, "You've certainly got a rapier-quick mind, you lovely thing." (But please don't call me *thing*.) A little imagination, and you will be home free. Incidentally, an attractive woman loves to hear compliments about her mind.

Is this agreeable?

If so, I will have my assistant update the TERMS AND CONDITIONS, and we can decide the all-important question of when. Due to unexpected cancellations, I'm free next Friday or Saturday if either of those works for you.

Please let me know soonest!
Tricia

Dear Tricia,

Although my defendant's life is on the line for a murder most likely committed by an off-duty cop, I have set aside my tedious analysis of trace fibers, witness statements, and possibly falsified police reports to contemplate "sweet nothings" that might be useful during our DINNER DATE.

My legal pad now contains fifty-seven (57) flattering remarks that I might toss out, in a seemingly sincere and off-handed manner, while we feast on a rack of Bumgardner's famous ribs. Once I memorize the list, I will be able to pick and choose and surprise you with the comments that seem most apt and likely to please you.

What if they number more than three? Am I allowed to exceed this arbitrary threshold?

Am I required to sign the TERMS AND CONDITIONS?

Insults May Vary

How about Friday?
Mark

Dear Mark,

Your sly eloquence always delights me. I hope, however, that your allusion to ribs does not imply any obligation on my part to eat them—since, as you might know, I consume only veggies and seafood and probably will order fish.

Re "sweet nothings": No limit applies. I asked for three as a target minimum, realizing that the number might be greater if additional compliments flow as part of the *natural* [my emphasis] course of conversation. A "sweet spot" of six or eight might be ideal to avoid the impression of "overdoing it."

Before you sign the TERMS AND CONDITIONS, please let me have my assistant deal with a few "i's" and "t's." We are mere hours away from a final draft!

Are you excited? In *Rheinhart v. Stimpson* (2012), a Virginia appellate court held (with Magnussen dissenting) that the initiating party should voice excitement at the opportunity to spend an evening with a desirable woman.

See you soon!
Tricia

Dear Tricia,

Please send along those revised TERMS AND CONDITIONS as soon as they are available. Given their length and complexity, I'd like adequate time to look them over prior to filing a plea on behalf of my luckless client, who is about to be railroaded as sure as the moon circles the earth.

Excited? Yes, I am extremely excited.

Speaking of the moon, I am sure Armstrong's trip took less time to plan.

Mark

Dear Mark,

Just to clarify your last note, I hope you did not mean to indicate that you are *sexually* excited.

California's Ninth Circuit has held, in *Lathrop v. Cunningham* (2014), that a man who communicates his sexual excitement to a woman by means of letter, email, or voicemail may be criminally guilty of harassment and/or liable for civil damages. In fact, given the escalating volume of our correspondence and our physical proximity at various times in the courthouse, I could probably make a solid case for stalking—not that I would.

Pending one last review, here is an updated copy of the TERMS AND CONDITIONS.

XOXO,

Tricia

Dear Tricia,

Why do I fear that you're filing these notes for purposes of future litigation?

For the record, my excitement about the DINNER DATE is strictly emotional. If there is a fine line between being emotionally engaged and being the sort of uber-lecherous, boner-wielding psychopath you seem to imagine most men to be—locked in an unceasing campaign to maneuver his well-engorged jackhammering equipment to the secret drilling site of a woman's ovaries—I have walked up to that line but have not touched it or strayed across it.

At this point, I would describe my under-utilized male member

Insults May Vary

as being as flaccid as a washcloth in a torrential downpour.

By the way, on page 22 of the updated TERMS AND CONDITIONS, I object to the new language saying I "shall extend my pinky from the stem of my cocktail glass with the air of a gentleman."

I do not extend my pinky, ever. No matter the occasion.

Anything else?

Mark

Dear Mark,

Might I remind you that royalty subscribes to the etiquette of the extended pinky, and that Prince Philip, the Duke of Edinburgh, was once famously photographed with his pinky ever-so-gracefully crooked from a glass of sherry—an image that, to me, exemplifies the very essence of nobility.

However, since apparently you are more of a "beer with the boys" guy, the offending language is removed.

Are you happy?

By the way, I've been dying for French cuisine. I hope it will not be too much trouble if we change the venue of the DINNER DATE to Chez Lalique.

Oui?

Tricia

Dear Tricia,

Chez Lalique? Well, if I sell my Audi, I'm sure we can dine there and still manage a nightcap.

Thank you re: the pinky language. When will I see the final TERMS AND CONDITIONS?

Mark

Dear Mark,

As a last failsafe, I ran the revised 46-page draft TERMS AND CONDITIONS by my friend Victoria Laskey, a brilliant woman who represented two of the early Cosby accusers. She noted that you and I completely overlooked one of the hot-button social issues of our time—the problem of *leering*.

Many a woman's romantic night has been wrecked by this deplorable practice. God forbid I should be telling some amusing tale or imparting insight on a political matter of wide interest, only to discover that your mind has disengaged and your head has swiveled to meet the eyes of an enticing temptress seated at another table.

Uuugh! I will not stand for it.

Attached are the final TERMS AND CONDITIONS, including the non-leering addendum that Laskey suggests. Please read it all carefully.

Once you've signed, the DINNER DATE is on!

Tricia

Dear Tricia,

Would you mind if we just meet for coffee instead?

Mark

Insults May Vary

Lesser Artists of the Renaissance

Rightly regarded as a glorious high-water mark of art and culture, the Renaissance was a curious time—bursting with creative élan and yet strangely overrated, its historical importance swollen almost to the point of caricature by aggressive post–Dark Ages marketing campaigns. Rome-based publicity giant Giuseppe, Luigi & Pepitone was known for booking its clients at galas, receptions, soirées, and even competitive dog shows as a means of entrée into the monied realms of the elite. Famously, Michelangelo was coerced into operating a weekly autograph booth in the Vatican's Piazza San Pietro. He spent every Saturday telling ribald stories and scrawling his herky-jerky signature for people in weird hats. At designated intervals, he would don a turban and try his hand at amateur fortune-telling. It is said that the master sculptor accurately predicted the events of May 11, 1523, when drunken rapscallions tarred and feathered nine members of the Holy See.

Undeniably, such crass self-promotion boosted the careers and reputations of a few so-called "geniuses"—Da Vinci was another one—while relegating scores of deserving rivals to the stinking garbage heap of oblivion. Honest scholars now concede the uncomfortable truth: that in many instances, these "lesser lights" were of far greater talent and vision than the marble-headed icons so blindly worshipped by modern critics.

Consider the following transcendent spirits, each supremely gifted, each now largely forgotten:

Ozzie the Greek

Born in poverty on the outskirts of Milan—he also died in poverty there—this swaggering, gap-toothed innovator was not actually named Ozzie, nor was he Greek; he adopted the persona to evade a series of larceny charges. He was in and out of jails and detention halls as a youth, a shiftless renegade who discovered an aptitude for painting one summer on the Amalfi Coast.

Never one for convention, Ozzie eschewed canvas and other media to invent, almost single-handedly, a style of face-painting lauded for its heavy, drippy viscosity and bold colors. His first subject was a tall, rather brawny mackerel fisherman whom he found lying asleep on a beach at Vietri sul Mare. Ozzie swooped in like a seabird, carrying a crock of pigment, and painted the fisherman's nose with what is now thought to have been a brilliant shade of blue—"to make it the nose of all noses," he later explained.

Sadly, his irascible and unappreciative subject (clearly not an art lover) sprang up and beat the living crap out of him, but Ozzie was undaunted. He spent much of the ensuing two years—his "blue period"—applying the same audacious hue to hundreds of unwitting snouts from Ravello to Positano. The second time his own nose was broken, he began to expand his palette, adding red, purple, green, orange, and fuchsia, and experimenting with ever-faster application techniques. Eventually, he learned to stage "darting artsy ambushes," the phrase he used (here translated to English) to describe the process of pouring paint into a bowl or cup and dumping it onto a target nose as he hurried past. Even at a slow trot, Ozzie was adept at hitting his mark, and yet he was content to allow color to follow its own course, "going whither and whence it will." Such artistic abandon gave Ozzie's work a winning degree of abstraction. He loved to see gooey rivulets of brilliant yellow or green transform the flesh-toned landscapes of human cheeks, mouths, and chins, and he spoke effusively about the "visual wonders" he created when a tsunami of golden orange flooded the finely bristled forest of a head of hair.

In his later years, following his release from prison, Ozzie the Greek became an influential originator of public performance art. He liked to load up a veritable lake of sloppy paint onto a flat, round tray—what we now would call a pizza pan—and carry it into a crowded marketplace. At an opportune moment, he would give it a mighty fling, Frisbee-style. The clothing of every unsuspecting passerby would serve as a potential canvas. "I start with a riot of colors," Ozzie once explained, "and sometimes I'm able to create a true actual riot, which always thrills me."

Benito Gigliotti

The so-called "Blind Sculptor of Naples"—though many claimed he could see well enough with his 20/70 vision and owlish spectacles—Gigliotti achieved a substantial following and ephemeral fame in the 1470s by mastering a technique he called *tactile fragmentary reductivism*, in which, with painstaking effort, he manually adhered his sculpting medium to the posed nude forms of his alluring young models.

Seizing a handful of fresh clay or his preferred medium, molten paraffin wax (cooling but still buttery soft), he would slather the substance onto the breast or thigh of a provocatively positioned female. Multiple applications would produce a surprisingly firm, durable "skin" with all the nuanced contours of the model herself.

Gigliotti spent weeks at a time assembling sections of these "erotic molds" into life-sized, fully realized figures that delighted members of Italy's ruling families. The artist's generous gifts to them effectively shielded him from the Church's draconian indecency laws. At the peak of Gigliotti's renown, his staunchest benefactors began gathering an enormous trove of his most ambitious sculptures—thousands in all. The plan was to create a permanent display: the world's first wax museum. A site was chosen overlooking the seacoast in Naples. The enormous edifice would have rivaled the mammoth Egyptian Library at Alexandria as one of history's most spectacular public venues.

Alas, the Great Naples Fire of 1794 not only destroyed the museum before its completion—it also consumed more than ninety percent of Gigliotti's most treasured works, reducing them to streaming wax puddles.

Carlo Campanello

A child prodigy, capable of computing ten-digit square roots in his head and fluent in eleven languages before he entered his teens, Campanello was an *intellect nonpareil*, in the estimable words of none other than Flaubert. The youth astounded his professors at university with such counterintuitive notions as solar fusion, gravitational lensing, and mass and energy being pretty much the same thing.

This incomparable polymath reached a crossroads at age twenty, when he was invited to collaborate with the ultimate scientific mentor, Galileo. "Together," the elder man promised, "we can unravel the secrets of the universe." But by then, Campanello was fixated on art—specifically, on the multitude of patterns that could be made by stringing together colorful wooden beads.

What Campanello realized was that a string scarcely the length of a man's arm could hold an astonishing number of possible bead configurations. He would put a red bead next to a blue one and then add a yellow—or a green. He mixed them willy-nilly in accordance with his own whims. Sometimes he would string together three or four orange ones, side by side, before deciding—aha!—I'll switch to purple right here! Or black! Or chartreuse! Every decision was a new and profound expression of his art. Just how the entire string turned out was anyone's guess!

Campanello's next glorious insight exemplified the sort of brain-on-fire hoo-boy brilliance that would someday put men on the moon. For he saw that the number of possible color juxtapositions would increase wildly if he laid out additional strings alongside the first. A red bead on one string might line up next to a blue bead on another. An orange might line up next to a green—or another orange. Viewed *en toto*, the effect was mosaic-like, magical.

Rejecting Galileo's offer, the headstrong Campanello retreated for months at a time into a dank, barren study, sketching diagrams by candlelight: rows of beads of varying lengths and configurations, matched this way and that. Two strings were good, three were even better. Why not six, seven, eight? Ten? Twelve?

In his journals, Campanello commented on the "new vistas of awareness" that accompanied these discoveries, the "mental pyrotechnics" that in a later era might have been labeled psychosis. He splurged by buying all the beads he could—from BeadWorks, from Beads R Us, from Antonio the bead-maker down the street—and, at desperate times, when bead shortages beset the Italian economy, he resorted to carving the little round devils himself.

Another critical matter was finding an optimal way to display the finished strings. Understandably, the artist was loath to leave them lying on a table or jumbled up in a bowl or underwear drawer. He usually hung them on the wall—expedient, but lacking panache. This is where, once again, the raging electrical storm that was Campanello's mind provided a way forward: a new insight struck him, a lightning bolt so blazingly bright that only other geniuses could appreciate it. Considering that fact, I have to ask that you continue reading only if you are a genius, too. Non-geniuses should stop immediately, because the nature of that extraordinary lightning-bolt insight is revealed in the next paragraph.

The wunderkind saw that certain instruments were not only aesthetically pleasing, but they were literally designed to hold an array of strings. Imagine the tremulous excitement as Campanello began arranging beads—mostly blue and orange—on the strings of a Stradivarius. Just how he obtained the instrument is unknown. What is recorded is that the artist purposely left significant gaps between the beads. This way, a skilled violinist could still play Paumann or DuFay. Believe it or not, those particular composers were said to sound a little better.

Spurred on by that triumph, Campanello soon went a step further by borrowing a Moretti Brothers harp (the big one, not the "family" model) from Dona Maria Gavriadora, the celebrated lead harpist of the Greater Venice Chamber Orchestra. It took three weeks and more than fifteen hundred beads for Campanello to transform the entire instrument with exactly the effect he wanted. Seen from across the room, the visual pattern of red, yellow, green, and gray beads resembled a bowl of rigatoni with a side salad—the artist's favorite meal. Western culture is poorer for the fact that no images of this work remain. Some sources, having researched it, say it might have compared favorably to Picasso's *Guernica*. A stretch, perhaps, but all available evidence suggests that Campanello's *Harp with Marinara Sauce* stirred strong emotions in those who saw it; certainly that was the case with Dona Maria herself. Upon the harp being returned to her, on the eve of her scheduled performance of the *Partite sopra Zefiro* at Talanini's, the harpist (also a former child prodigy) was moved to tears. According to one contemporary account, her sobbing lasted less than a minute before the normally docile virtuoso hauled off and gave Campanello a whack with the flat of her hand—"a slap heard all the way to Sicily," as the *Venice Canal-Herald* later dubbed it.

Today, an original Campanello "bead job" would fetch upwards of $10 million or more—if one could be found. Art historian J. McClausen Carmichael commented, "We'll see a woolly mammoth first. Or a Bigfoot on water skis."

Sylvia Pietra-Manzini

Perhaps the greatest of the "Distaff Dozen," the elite female artists and thinkers scattered across the vestiges of the old Roman Empire, this elfin product of Palermo labored as an impoverished washerwoman until her 47th birthday, when she cursed a pair of tattered socks, chucked away her laundry basket, and became one of the age's most prolific specialty artists—her particular niche being that staple of Renaissance paintings and sculpture: the halo.

A Harvard study reports that 698,740 halos were painted on commissioned art pieces during Pietra-Manzini's halcyon days, perhaps half of them by the artist herself. Even irrefutable legends such as Titian and Botticelli struggled with the simple elliptical symmetries that a convincing halo required. Often, they would enlist Pietra-Manzini to add—anonymously—the crowning halo or halos to an otherwise finished work, a *pièce de résistance* that Ravenstiehl likens to the cherry atop a banana split.

A halo painted by Pietra-Manzini was said to be "the essence of quintessence... [an] exquisite oblong loop of incandescent holy rapture," according to *Fabian's Complete Unabridged Halos and Angel Wings*. It is hard to overstate the ardor of Pietra-Manzini's fans, many of whom came to see her as a living embodiment of Heaven's glory. A number of fanatical admirers, including Pope Sixtus IV, even claimed to see mystical evidence of the fact. Every so often, when the evening light was exactly right, the woman's aura seemed to emerge—an ethereal glow, fully translucent—and within moments, if you kept looking, you would begin to observe (according to witnesses) a bona fide holy halo (the real thing!) hovering like the golden rings of Saturn above her strangely elongated noggin.

While such purported sightings are usually written off as apocrypha—"unadulterated balderdash," in Reva Clementine's frank assessment—the increasingly eccentric, cantankerous artist did take to wearing a teakwood, gold-painted facsimile halo supported by a rigid wire and corset; its presence, even at formal banquets and royal receptions, inspired her well-known nicknames: "The Old Kook," "Lady Kook," and "Cuckoo Bird."

Luciano "Luther" Lazzeri

Few men of any era possessed Lazzeri's remarkable measure of good looks, charm, and capacity for befriending a Who's Who of living legends. Add to that his own ridiculous overabundance of God-given talent, and Lazzeri's success seemed assured. To imagine him a toothless, broken-down wreck, begging on the streets of Milan, was inconceivable—until it happened.

Historians debate whether Lazzeri was aided or impeded by his long apprenticeship under Leonardo da Vinci, whom he met at a bread market in Florence. Barely seventeen but bristling with ideas and ambition, Lazzeri quickly became a trusted sounding board as the great master thought through some of the most heralded artworks in history. Among them was an oversized painting, begun circa 1495, that da Vinci intended to call *Breakfast with Jesus*.

The ever-confident upstart immediately challenged his mentor: "Why breakfast? And why do you want him eating with a bunch of thuggish gladiators? It is said that such exchanges occasionally became heated; da Vinci was touchy, at times. Yet out of the yin and yang of their clashing visions emerged a better painting: the beautifully composed canvas, featuring a dozen of Christ's disciples, known as *The Last Supper*.

Lazzeri's advisory role was equally essential some years later as da Vinci struggled to complete a portrait of the wealthy noblewoman Lisa del Giocondo.

"My God, she looks dour," Lazzeri remarked upon seeing the nearly finished painting. "You couldn't give her a smile?"

Da Vinci became defensive. "She's a serious woman. She's very important."

To which Lazzeri could only shake his head. "She looks like somebody killed her cat."

Da Vinci's last-minute tweaks helped to render *The Mona Lisa* the most famous painting of all time, though it did little to enhance Lazzeri's own career. He was, during this period, developing a style that would later be characterized as impressionism. He caused a brief sensation with a grinning woman's portrait he called *The Mona Maria*, but da Vinci saw it as an audacious rip-off. The two men fell out, and Lazzeri drifted south to Rome, where he divided time between sketching tourists for pocket money and assisting Michelangelo.

Toward the end of Michelangelo's arduous commission at the Sistine Chapel, Lazzeri won a contract of his own to paint the ceiling of the dining hall of the Greater Rome Supper Club. The job took seven years, inasmuch as the dining hall was huge, seating over four hundred people. Sparing not a single flowing color or curlicue, Lazzeri brought to life—in astounding detail—an extravagant scene (one hundred and sixty feet long) of ravenous dinner patrons devouring everything from cheese ravioli to beef shanks.

The self-proclaimed prophet Saldoman, who helped prepare for the public opening, hailed it as the finest example of art ever created—surpassing even Michelangelo's spectacular ceiling—more vivid, more ornate, superior in both composition and grandeur.

Tragically, only two days before the unveiling was to occur, a grease fire in the kitchen caused the supper club to burn down.

The entire ceiling was destroyed.

Lazzeri subsequently murdered the bumbling jackass who caused the fire but served only two years in prison due to a temporary-insanity ruling. He drifted between Milan and Florence for the rest of his years, mumbling in Latin and living on handouts from strangers.

David Ferrell

Reviews of My Finest Craft Wines

Long ago, I broke with the purists who still dominate the ancient art of winemaking. Their rules and customs are maddening. They place enormous emphasis on the process—on "doing it right"—often without regard for the real priority: taste. Think about it. You're trying to coax a drinkable beverage from the sour, rotting carcass of a pinot noir grape. Why would you not add a dash of Tabasco sauce, if it helps? Or stir in a small packet of brown gravy?

Believe me, in my pursuit of the perfect craft wines, I have explored many unconventional methods—including, I admit, some real doozies—and along the way discovered some very excellent secrets. I'll share two, just to illustrate my style. You can try these yourself:

- For a distinctive, zesty Chianti, forget about oak barrels. Age your wine in a leak-proof plywood box. After ten days, toss in a Snickers bar or a handful of Reese's Pieces, plus a pinch of sea salt.
- To create my signature Malbec, augment the grapes with bits of carrot, sweet potato, and cremini mushrooms. Age in charred dogwood. After three weeks, filter out the veggies (I suggest using a small net of the type made for goldfish), then stir thoroughly with a fully cooked, well-seasoned turkey drumstick. (Ideally, bake the drumstick using Shake 'N Bake Spicy Cajun mix, if available. Not every store has it.)

Insults May Vary

Narrow-minded dolts would love to shutter my small craft label, Wendigo, and no doubt also put a slug in my head. I can only point to the success of my many blends and varietals. In response to one especially vocal critic (the flaming assbite Len Braxton), I invited an expert from *Wine Gastronome*, the highly regarded specialty magazine, to taste-test a selection of my premium offerings. Keep in mind that *Wine Gastronome* has a well-documented bias toward major commercial labels. Even so, I gladly present the full text of the thumbnail reviews written by the magazine's own J. Radcliffe Souza. I haven't changed a word!

Wendigo Vineyards Cabernet Sauvignon, 2019 — A highly viscous, syrupy wine with overpowering tannins and strong hints of pomegranate, black cherry, sweet gum, and gum arabic beneath a complex veneer of cedar bark, ginger root, and Worcestershire sauce. Robust and uncompromising, with lingering top notes of raspberry Danish, this truly unique spirit manages a long, tart finish with a bowl-'em-over aftertaste of rubbing alcohol. *29 points.*

Wendigo Vineyards Chardonnay, 2024 — This cloudy, sediment-rich white attacks the palate with a bold, almost harrowing array of influences. There are emerging high notes of lemongrass, buckwheat, and—honest to God—Rondele cheese spread. The wine's exceptional minerality lingers in the mouth and recalls the chalky aftertaste of having a cavity drilled. The finish revs up with surprising acidity, resulting in the long-lasting, not-entirely-pleasant sensation of the tongue and throat going numb. *17 points.*

Wendigo Vineyards Riesling, 2025 — Notable for a distinctive bouquet combining spritely lime and honeydew scents with a thick, pervasive catfish smell, this audacious rendition of a Riesling comes on strong with a startling undercurrent of candied yam and cauliflower. The mellow middle range meanders among hints of cinnamon, blueberry, paprika, and French onion soup. A lively finish introduces late top notes of oak and redwood plank. *22 points.*

Wendigo Vineyards Côtes du Rhône, 2023 — Perhaps no prior rip-off of the French appellation dares such an eclectic convergence of elements: bitter tannins, turbulent dashes of cherry, black currant, and soy sauce, and a full mid-range of more complex flourishes, highlighted by evanescent notes of garlic, curry powder, and anchovy paste. A full-bodied bouquet evokes a hot August in an unvented greenhouse; the garish finish ends with a queasy blast of mesquite BBQ chicken wing. *16 points.*

Wendigo Vineyards Malbec, 2025 — An initial impression of gustatory harmony vanishes like cotton candy in the rain as rich, chocolatey grape flavors succumb to an onslaught of ickiness. The wine's emphatic minerality hints at concrete dust or powdered brick. Subtle notes of carrot and mushroom give way to a putrid infusion of sweet potato, further aggravated by a foul (fowl?) undercurrent of flame-grilled poultry. The finish, which can't occur soon enough, would best involve spitting out this gruesome abomination into the kitchen sink. *14 points.*

Wendigo Vineyards (Red) Zinfandel, 2024 — A fitting wine to conclude our sampling, drawing together a smorgasbord of disparate and incompatible flavors into another dense and unsettling grape stew. This concoction—fortunately unprecedented in all the world—begins with harsh cayenne, horseradish, and mustard influences and builds to a sharp, metallic mélange—do we detect aluminum foil?—shrouded in a faint bouquet of chlorine. Undercurrents of Hollandaise sauce and curdled milk hasten a long, acrid finish that lingers forever, even after a hasty glass of water. This opaque zin feels greasy and somehow eel-like on the palate; it virtually slithers down the throat. *8 points.*

Well-meaning friends have carped at what they perceive as a dismissive or derogatory tone in a few of these reviews, failing to grasp the larger picture—that it takes time for new creative directions to gain popularity. Ratings points notwithstanding, I sense success in disrupting an overly hidebound field: I've opened a small crack toward necessary tectonic shifts in the winemaking landscape.

Toward that end, and in the same spirit of innovation, my newly formed Wendigo Foods division will soon be reimagining many of the classic dishes we all grew up with. Not to disclose too much too soon, let me just say that I have many fish to fry. To wit, I've never understood why trout is so seldom served as a dessert with whipped cream and chocolate frosting. Have you tried it? And is there some taboo that forbids stuffing a turkey with lemon Jell-O?

I plan to find out. Subscribe online for updates.

Dr. Cronquist's Final Paper

Perhaps no professor in Harvard's long history was as pompous, eccentric, and self-absorbed as Dr. Alton Cronquist, the celebrated linguist who was finally forced into retirement at age ninety-six. "The Old Codger" had become an iconic figure, shuffling across campus with his all-chrome walker, his high shock of unruly white hair blowing in the cool Cambridge breeze. "Father Time" was one of his nicknames. Many recent students simply referred to him as "that weird old fart" or "Dr. Freaky Bones."

Cronquist's greatest legacy may be his vast, albeit highly uneven, body of written work. A seven-time Nobel Prize nominee—he never won—he authored a staggering 849 academic papers over seven decades. His final scholarly tract was an apt swan song, "a stunning intellectual tour-de-force by a true American genius," in the bravura language of Cronquist's own cover letter. Various journal editors who reviewed (and rejected) the piece labeled it "unbelievable," "really out there," "an arrogant senile maverick's deluded fever dream."

Trimmed to a fraction of its original length, but otherwise unedited, Cronquist's impassioned treatise, *Roots of Select Semantic Phraseologies*, is published here for the first time.

By Dr. Alton T. Cronquist, PhD

Dim-bulb dinosaurs of academia like nothing better than to convene in some dank institution, crack open an unabridged dictionary, and pontificate about the obscure origins of recondite words and phrases. *Très jejune!* However, insofar as the practice brings no abject danger to others—especially me—I am loath to inveigh ridicule. I would merely point out that such brazen intellectual posturing (let's call it what it is) is woefully—and I mean woefully—inadequate to achieve the real goal: a deeper grasp of jargon's myriad spurious epigrams and epistolaries. Too many of these remain hanging, like ever-dangling participles—or like the sweet kumquats of Tantalus—just beyond the begging fingers of our cerebral reach.

Fortunately, despite my inveterate self-styled modesty, I can admit to having mastered the means to access all manner of "lost" knowledge—including roots and corollaries about specific English-language derivations—through a method at once mysterious and mystical.

My technique, based on autodidactic principles invented by the Druids (or possibly by Sumerian potentates before them), is one I confected during long, extremely fallow creative periods of my post-pubescence—a time that is far from over, incidentally. Through this lugubrious practice, I can direct my mind—which fluctuates nimbly from alpha to delta and even theta rhythms—into a state of focused, or heuristical, contemplation. The result is extraordinary: the aegis becomes ritualized, the tchotchkes nearly inviolate, and by powers of sheer intuition and trenchant intellect (I've been shown to possess one of the most trenchant hyper-intellects ever ostracized), I am able to glean, somehow, without access to any form of text or internet (which don't have the information, anyway), fundamental truths about our ever-evolving language that might never otherwise be discerned.

Let me repeat that: *fundamental truths about our ever-evolving language that might never otherwise be discerned!*

What truths? Consider a term at random: *wicca*, a word frequently associated with the conjuring of magic—or *magick*—by harnessing the quintessence of elemental forces: fire, wind, earth, and the raging tides. While the etymology of *wicca* remains elusive to linguists—and even to the most brilliant ornithologists (which is pretty obvious, since it's not in their field!)—I was able to enter a trance-like panaisch wherein my cerebral plasmus, that ineffable essence Jung called the collective *hyberstalsis*, plumbed time and space and brought back the miasma of a core root.

This work took place in a simple earthen room in the hill country of Austin, Texas, during a three-week planetary transit spanning parts of July and August of 2019. The *husticus* focused on a process of elimination, wherein my alternate mind *surrierred* a phalanx of terms not claded to the word *wicca* as we use it today.

On the fourth or fifth day, I reached an insight which illuminated—quite clearly—that *wicca* and its antecedents have absolutely no connection whatsoever to the phonetically similar term *whiplash*. In a similar vein, I have defined a *truncas interregnum* between *wicca* and a host of other thoracic nouns and phrases, including *whistle stop*, *wisteria*, *elephant*, *lima bean*, *lamppost*, *kneecap*, and *polystyrene*. (The full list of *interregnaeia* is on my website: www.truncas.interregnum/wicca/listefine-/root/fullquery=question??/massiveintellect.com.)

Therefore, I state emphatically: Anyone who claims that *wicca* is derived from *whiplash* or the *wisteria* vine—as I'm sure J. Wexler Cartwright, that idiot, would argue—is not only mistaken but may be regarded as a deliberate hoaxster or a *petite-au-douche* ignoramus. Only a *sub-puissant* fool would cling to that miscreant viewpoint.

Which brings us now to the very heart of modern English, *en toto*, by which I refer to that lovely, cruel, laborious string of elemental building blocks, the alphabet itself. Sad to say, most modern scholars are still in kindergarten with respect to the alphabet. (*Kindergarten*, now *there's* a word—see my paper of Jan. 23, 1977, in *Roots & Adverbs*, in which I deconstruct *kindergarten* and refute the nonsense promulgated by the ostentatious quack Dr. Jackie Osborne.) I'll give my rivals this much: Most of them can recite, from memory, all twenty-six letters—usually in the proper order.

Insults May Vary

Whoop-dee-doo!

But do they truly *know* those potent symbols the way a Sioux hunter knows the ways of the wolverine? I herald this corollary: Poppycock! Don't be fooled by the self-aggrandizing cognoscenti, as personified by the slick-as-glass Dr. Silas R. M. Massengale—another of my antagonists—that strutting ass. I swear to God, you could kick back and, as the stoners say, waft a gnarly reefer with Noam Chomsky himself—as I've done many, many times—and you'll likely hear the same flip rejoinders about alpha meaning A and beta meaning B, and so on, as if that superficial answer (no doubt delivered from deep in a blue tetrocannabinoidal haze) even comes close to addressing the real puzzler: *To wit, why* (!) does alpha stand for a letter shaped like a small mountain cabin, etc., etc., *ad infinitum nolo dictum*?

Chomsky = chomp skee = chomp sky = bite sky = bite, bit, will bite, bitten. Chomp, chomp, chomp.

Elucidating madly, I entered the heuristical gravitas during a 2021 visit to Esalen—the famed mind institute in California's Big Sur—where my frissionary powers were put to the test, big-time, by greater minds than yours, dear reader, that's for damn sure. I say this as stipulated background: Right at that moment, beguiled by the hypnotic yin-yang of a queen's cut amethyst swinging on a jute cord, I entered a panaischistic *husticus* that lasted a full thirty-nine hours, enabling me to dictate—à la Edgar Cayce—a gnostic treasure trove of derivational insights. One of these, naturally, addressed *alphabet*.

Alpha (as my deep insight revealed) comes to us from the ancient utterance—not a word, per se—*alffa*, a noise produced deep in the throat by the Jumanjari peoples of pre-historic Miami—not the Miami you may know, but the vast African anticline later appellenated as the Great Rift Valley, a fractious and vertiginous *crayhole* of early *Homophobus sapiens* culture.

The Jumanjari, of course, were nomads; they subsisted largely on snakes and beetles, often accompanied by a rich shot of wildebeest blood—which tells you all you need to know about the desperate scavenging they endured to keep their dear hearts beating. Eventually, these shoeless (and sockless) *primitivas* extrapolated north, transfixing the term to nascent agrarian tribes in lower Mesopotamia. There, *alffa* gave us the common word *alfalfa*—a dry and unappetizing crop, but better than eating beetles, eh? Harvested alfalfa, piled in conical mounds, would look very familiar to a first-grade student staring at a capital A on the chalkboard.

Here again, I must re-state the *truncas interregnum*, enjoining the brute fact that *alpha*, while phonetically co-resplendent, has absolutely no common associative root with *alabaster*, *à la mode*, *elephant*, nor, for that matter, with any of the major quadrupeds. (If you thought so, I pity your ignorance, so emblematic of today's generalized slipshod erudition—ugh!)

The term is also wholly unrelated to *whale shark*, *altruism*, *sinus cavity*, and *windshield wiper*.

Bet, the dependent ordinal of *alphabet*, is a far easier cipher, deriving (as the *husticus* revealed) from the traditional Sanskrit liturgical axiom *betabunchen*, meaning (in the broadest reasonable translation) *to take a grave risk*. I won't belabor the equistatically self-evident point that the syllable *bet* conveys a gamble—which, by the way, you might regret once you've blown the rent money on the New York Jets or Denver Broncos. *Cravat emperor!*

By way of which: fuck the ecumenical bastard who instigated me to lay down eight large on the Packers last week. Burn in hell, you crenellated assbite.

Anyway, ideally, at this point, I would ossify the catalytic nomenclature by laying out, symbol by symbol, the entire grammarian root structure—so to speak—of the familiar Latin/English *stæfræw*. Don't doubt that some embodiment is in order: that trenchant string of symbols might be as baffling and incongruous as any on Earth. Rest assured, there are conundrums within conundrums concealed in that chorus line of arcs and squiggles, as surely as indigenous vertebrae consigned the shape and function of the untamed early creatures that slithered out of the primordial muck.

    I hope to postulate further on these linguistic details once the relevant thoughts crystallize. Regrettably, that has not yet occurred. Even abetted by the rancid chemical compounds of the psilocybin fungus, I've found—during repeated attempts—that much of the *husticus* has become hazy, like a dumpy housemaid viewed through the refractive striations of a shower door. Sadly, maintaining the *panaisch* is often akin to sustaining a quality Wi-Fi signal when all you've got is a cheap garage-office router—and what you want, the information you seek, is in a relay link stuffed inside a tin can. And where's the tin can? That little fucker's in orbit somewhere around Jupiter.

David Ferrell

FILM REVIEW:
The Sad and Hilarious Brilliance of 'The Elevator'

It was tragic, of course: Eight thousand priceless Iraqi statues, dating to the dawn of civilization, crushed by steamrollers and shoveled into a mineshaft—for no other reason than they had been featured on U.S. television. So it has been throughout the ages—masterworks defaced, discredited, or condemned to obscurity because of senseless political squabbles. Once again, we must hold a pillow to our faces and scream.

The outrage this time involves what is probably—in fact, almost certainly—the greatest feature film ever made: the profound, emotionally moving, alternately comic and wrenching, yet finally redeeming and uplifting (albeit slightly sardonic) Spanish epic *Encerrado en un Ascensor*, or *Stuck in an Elevator*.

Not even the makers of the film profess to understand the decades-old dispute that has kept the four-hour-and-twenty-nine-minute drama bottled up, unavailable for public viewing except on a single private screen in a Madrid mansion. Commercial release is impossible, thanks to the all-time mother of a pissing match between the Spanish government's cultural affairs bureau and the quasi-autonomous *Cinemática de Artistas Asociación*, a body now almost entirely controlled by a faction of Basque dory fishermen.

What a crime. The movie that languishes would make American classics such as *Citizen Kane* and *Gone With the Wind* seem like disjointed horror shows patched together by freshman film-school hacks. A noted French critic, fortunate enough to see *Elevator* during a small, specially arranged screening for foreign writers (which I also attended), emerged blinking back tears and exclaiming, "Nothing can be this good. No one will ever again approach it." Journalists came away sobbing—or, if they weren't sobbing, they were laughing. Or, if they weren't sobbing or laughing, they had that look—that mix of sorrow and laughter, tinged with deeper emotions, along with the secret knowledge that important people around them had been moved to tears. Or to laughter.

A writer from Bangladesh may have said it best in four simple words: "I am rice noodles." (In Bangladeshi, the expression is analogous to our phrase, "I'm totally floored.")

Never mind the spate of elevator films released in recent years, including that fright-night flick by M. Night Shyamalan. This Spanish wonder—shot on a budget of under $30,000—is not to be confused with any of them. Skeptics ask how a film made for so little can elicit such extraordinary praise. The answer is obvious: in filmmaking, as in any art, genius finds a way. Genius doesn't require a huge budget, superstar actors, or CGI; it doesn't kowtow to egomaniacal studio heads or get swayed by the mood of the moment. Where lesser minds see constraints, genius sees the full gamut of possibilities and exploits them with a sure-handed panache that brings fire to the screen and makes the audience stand up and roar—as indeed they did. They stood and roared and wept and cackled like maniacs.

Oh, my God, I wish I could do justice to what I witnessed that night.

Which brings me to the film's director, Jaime D'Ambrusco-Lopez (*Streets of Sleet*, *Lorenzo's Dilemma*), a twenty-two-year-old wunderkind who, in just his third picture, showed cajones the size of medicine balls by shooting the entire four-plus hours in a single take—and entirely within the confines of a motionless, eight-by-eight-foot elevator.

D'Ambrusco-Lopez might have been forgiven for employing flashbacks or cutaways to shift the action outside the lift, especially since so much of the movie—nearly two hours—occurs in complete blackness. From where springs such hutzpah? This is a director whose track record wasn't exactly transcendent. *Streets*, though brilliant in its own right, was panned by critics who found it dark and abstruse. It lasted scarcely a week in theaters during its Europe-only release. *Dilemma* was more fully evolved, revealing greater glimpses of D'Ambrusco-Lopez's virtuosity, but again, audiences were sparse—and the film, which played only in Spain and Angola, was ultimately blamed for the bankruptcy of Carga Toro Studios.

Spanish film insiders speculate that the reclusive director, who routinely declines interviews, simply doesn't care whether critics or audiences embrace his avant-garde style. "March to his own drummer?" Oliver Stone asked rhetorically, when D'Ambrusco-Lopez's name came up at Cannes. "Christ, man, I think the guy marches to a bagpipe band and a choir of Inuit throat singers. Marches is probably the wrong word. I picture him shambling, skipping—maybe stopping along the way to do an occasional cartwheel."

"D'Ambrusco-Lopez, es los frijoles!" screamed a headline in the *Tijuana Times-Telegraph*, which sent a correspondent to the screening. He's the beans! His flawless direction, coupled with Sergio Acevedo's remarkable script, resulted in a film so taut, so compelling, that it feels like less than an hour. Forty-five minutes, tops. No wonder: Acevedo, the sole credited screenwriter, reportedly got help from nine other master scribes who reworked the story at least two dozen times.

"The most perfect thing ever written," in essayist George McCord's words, was made all the more provocative by D'Ambrusco-Lopez's inspired decision to overdub the dialogue so that it's heard in three languages at once—Spanish, English, and Cantonese. Amazingly, the human mind distills the meaning. The resultant cacophony, instead of causing confusion, actually heightens the dramatic arc to an almost unbearable tension.

Insults May Vary

Without spoiling the plot, let me say the action begins when a motor apparently malfunctions due to years of neglect. I say *apparently* because there are hints that rodents may have been gnawing on old, cloth-insulated wiring. (How their involvement is surmised is one of the cleverest bits.) Whatever the root cause, the elevator car stops abruptly, high in a bank building, trapping fourteen people inside. This motley group includes a shrieking baby, a pickpocket, a pregnant spiritualist who reads Tarot cards, and a white-bearded African who is believed to be infected with the Ebola virus. It turns out—one of many startling twists—that his worrisome nosebleed resulted from being smacked in the face by a glass door in the lobby. But that revelation comes later. *(Spoiler alert: I probably just spoiled that for you.)*

Already you can see the potential for drama, but believe me, you are not smart enough (nor was I) to anticipate the manifold directions this exquisitely layered plot takes as it touches upon subjects from rhinoceros mating to incontinence. I laughed out loud when Renée, the bank's young new-accounts administrator, tries to do jumping jacks, and I nearly split a gut when someone off-screen with a megaphone—presumably on the floor below—yells out, "Is anybody in there?"

Oh, my Lord. *Anybody in there?*

Of course, the film derives most of its power from other emotions—anger, jealousy, poignancy, compassion, and lust—that explode at climactic moments. At the point where Vincente, the half-blind handyman, whips out a hammer from his toolbelt and cracks a moaning Miguel upside the head, the audience gasped and even cried out—some with horrified disapproval, and some because, Jesus Christ Almighty, I've literally never seen anything so uproariously funny.

Tempers explode—no surprise—and the film depicts a sort of chaos *organisé*, with the African man bleeding again, the baby wetting itself, and a claustrophobic tourist from Ireland losing her last Valium down a crack in the floor. *(Spoiler alert: You won't think it slipped through a crack, but it did.)* I won't say what happens next as the blackout sets in, but D'Ambrusco-Lopez manages to control these various elements like Yo-Yo Ma sawing out Vivaldi on his cello.

Just when our nerves are stretched out like snake hide on a tanning shed—we're wondering who will live, or if they'll all die—Vincente pipes up in his husky baritone: *"Who cut the cheese?"*

Then we are on the rack again, half-expecting, half-fearing that the Tarot seer will go into labor. Miguel's panic attack is an instant classic, punctuated brilliantly by a second, vigorous hammer blow to the noggin. The sex scene between Margo, the paraplegic, and Dmitri, the Russian diplomat, which begins during the first blackout, might be the finest love sequence ever shot—bold without being salacious, innocent and somehow searingly hot, and, given the lovers' predicament, frantically awkward. The tenor shifts perceptibly once the lights come back on, with Millie, the old woman, being drawn into her first tryst in thirty years, completing a strangely satisfying—and I don't say that lightly—*ménage à trois*, which becomes an orgy on a psychological level: a sort of letting go, en masse, of accepted cultural norms. The vicarious fulfillment of yearnings that have built from the opening frame.

D'Ambrusco-Lopez's masterpiece is a rousing, eerie homage to both the scream-a-minute horror genre and the languid melodramas that the French and Norwegians used to do so well. If I have any quibble at all—which I don't—it's that I wanted more: more of Miguel madly punching the *LOBBY* button; more of Margo's tearful wailing; and certainly more of B.J. Bustamonte's riveting musical score.

The unknown Bustamonte, another prodigy—just nineteen—might have dulled the film's razor edge by succumbing to conventional instrumentation, but instead he employed crowbars, saws, sheet metal, and even cordless power tools to instill the film with booming, hammering, and grinding sounds, interspersed with the occasional well-timed screech. The period of loud radio static that dominates the middle act finally gives way to a staccato succession of high-pitched hydraulic noises—the kind you hear

Insults May Vary

when the auto shop is screwing on your lug nuts. It's yet another touch that feels almost divinely inspired. Several audience members were visibly moved.

You might imagine that the elevator motor is finally repaired—but, as I discovered, this isn't so easy! *(Spoiler alert: Tomasino Motors went out of business decades ago!)* I cannot, in good conscience, even hint at how the crisis is resolved, in hopes that the legal skirmish will end and *Elevator* finally gets the worldwide exposure it deserves.

Be assured that if and when you are ever able to see this remarkable movie, you will emerge wet-eyed with relief, joy, and utter shock after the solution presents itself—completely out of left field—bizarre and yet logical and, more than anything else, *perfect*, like *Elevator* itself.

David Ferrell

Can This Marriage Endure?

No one can doubt the power of the printed word to shape the course of human lives. If, however, I'm wrong and doubters exist—shame on those cynical dolts. They should take a hard look at the syndicated advice column *Can This Marriage Endure?*, as written by the wise but forever anonymous "Ms. Matrimony" in the old *San Diego Sun-Crier*.

Launched in 1971, the popular column ran weekly for thirty-six years before the daily folded in 2007. There's no telling how many couples chose to stay together—or divorce amid a firestorm of acrimony, accusations, and lawsuits—based on the penetrating insights of a writer who never even met the people involved. It's intriguing to wonder: whatever became of those anguished souls who turned to Ms. Matrimony as the final arbiter of where their life paths should go?

Let's examine some cases.

Dear Ms. Matrimony,

Sometimes I feel like I don't know my husband anymore. We've been married for a very long time—three years. At first, Michael was loving and generous. An ideal husband. Come to find out, he's not Michael at all. Tells me one day, out of the blue, that his name is really Willis. *Willis?* I'm floored. *Willis?* I'm allowed to call him Will, he tells me. Or Fred. I try them both a few times—and I'm leaning toward Fred, a nice, decent name—and then

whammo! Oh, my freakin' God—*WHAMMO!* I'm blindsided. He says his name is really Gary! And later on, he says it's Theodore. A few weeks go by and it's Roland. And this guy Roland has a criminal rap sheet in Missouri and South Dakota. I had been hoping to start a family with this man. Should I go ahead or reconsider?
—**Baffled in Baltimore**

Dear Baffled,

I checked, and your husband's real name is Conrad. No, I mean it's Ivanhoe. What I'm saying, my dear lady, is that I know this clown about as well as you do. If you're wanting to start a crime family, he sounds perfect. Otherwise, dump this bastard. Get this joker out of your life by any means necessary.

How things worked out:

Months after appearing in Ms. Matrimony's column, Baffled took a trip with her husband to Coral Gables, Florida, on the pretext of celebrating their fourth wedding anniversary. According to authorities, while on a rented catamaran, the woman spiked Roland's drink and wrestled his unconscious body overboard— resulting in him being attacked and devoured by sharks. Baffled gave birth to her first child that same year in the medical ward of a federal penitentiary. Her son Ivanhoe is being raised by her parents.

Dear Ms. Matrimony,

Everyone says Jake, my husband, is a "super nice guy," and I guess it's true, but he has several annoying personal habits that drive me insane. For one thing, he is always cracking his knuckles. He cracks his knuckles at the dinner table, watching TV, and yakking on the phone. He must crack his knuckles two thousand times a day. His knuckles make a loud "pop-gun" sound. Even when I'm upstairs, I can hear him in the bathroom, blowing his nose and cracking his knuckles. That's the other thing—he blows his nose a tremendous amount. Morning, noon, and night, he blows his nose and cracks those damn knuckles. His nose makes a low honk-honky sound when he blows it, like a goose. You'd think I'd finally get some relief at night, but he's also an extremely loud snorer. Oh, my God, he sounds like a machine gun. I think I'm on Omaha Beach. I don't even want to mention his dirtier habits. Well, one is taking wax out of his ears when guests are over. I've tried talking to him, but nothing works. Honestly, I feel like shooting him sometimes, I really do. Would I be considered a "dirty slut," a "fucking bitch," or a "horrible person" if I moved out and never saw this repulsive freakazoid again?

—**Going Berserk in Newkirk**

Dear Berserk,

I have to smile, comparing your hellacious days and nights to my own complete tranquility, unspoiled by even a single unwanted sound as I relax to the soft strains of Miles Davis's horn or Keith Jarrett's piano solos. I can't blame you one bit for wanting to shoot the obnoxious freak. Good God Almighty, just a few hours of what you're putting up with and I'd be shopping for a gun. Or rigging up a car bomb for him. Now, don't get me wrong—I'm not advocating that you murder your husband. In fact, I want to make that clear: Do NOT murder your husband! Leaving him is another matter. Get out. Just go. It's better to be a horrible person or a dirty slut—which you may or may not be—than to go on suffering such torment.

How things worked out:

Going Berserk murdered her husband. Eleven months after the publication of her letter, she fashioned a bomb using nails, explosives, and a pressure-sensitive triggering device and rigged it to a toilet. When her husband sat down, he went up like a Titan missile, his head knocking a clean round hole in the ceiling. A severed leg landed in the bathtub. Going Berserk succeeded in fleeing the country and is rumored to be living in either Borneo or Papua New Guinea.

Dear Ms. Matrimony,

Sadly, my wife and I seem to be growing apart. I can trace the problem back to a period a few years ago when I was screaming at her a lot. Her hair, clothes, her irritating little habits—I'd yell like a maniac over anything, totally my fault, until eventually she divided the house into two sides, hers and mine. There was a line painted through the kitchen and I wasn't supposed to cross it. Then she got a whole separate place, and we'd meet once or twice a month for coffee. I worked on my temper, hoping to recapture the love, but one time at Starbucks I chewed her out something awful when she got crumbs all over the table—and wouldn't you know it, she moved to another city! A year's gone by and I heard from her sister that now she's living with a cop. A *cop!* Naturally, I went ballistic—Britt is my wife! I tried calling and the number was no good. The last address she gave me turned out to be a muffler shop where they never even heard of her. Assuming I can track her down, should I threaten her with divorce? I sure would like to beat the crap out of that cop! If I physically go get her, is it technically kidnapping if we're still legally married?
—**Abandoned in Abilene**

Dear Abandoned,

You sound like a sensible type. Think for a moment and you'll realize that Britt's evasive actions are a not-so-subtle cry for your attention. You indicate, in "Addendum No. 3" to your letter, that you are "pretty certain" she now resides in Portland, Maine—more than two thousand miles away. I'm sure she feels that enormous physical and emotional distance in every fiber of her being. It is natural for a woman alone in a strange town to take in a cop as a boarder, for personal protection. That's all it is. Keep the faith and ignore her. Before long, her intense longing for you will bring her back into the fold without any overt effort on your part. One day, she will magically appear on your doorstep, begging for your strong hand—your tough, he-man love.

How things worked out:

Abandoned spent four solid months giving Britt the silent treatment. Eventually, though, he disregarded Ms. Matrimony's wise counsel and took action—selling the house, quitting his job, and moving to Maine. For the better part of three years, the lovelorn hubby searched for his prodigal wife on every street and in every bar, café, grocery store, and back alley of Portland. A costly private detective helped ascertain the startling fact that Britt had actually gone to Portland, *Oregon,* not Maine. Once again, Abandoned pulled up stakes and moved. It took two more years—and the last of his savings—to locate the now-pregnant Britt, who had changed her name to Louise and was still living with the cop and their two young daughters. Soon afterward, Abandoned was arrested and imprisoned for attacking a parking enforcement officer with a crowbar.

Dear Ms. Matrimony,

My husband is no fun. He's just not. He lies around watching dumb-ass TV shows, never takes me out, never goes to restaurants or out dancing. Part of the problem is his age—he's 87—and he has a bad hip, chronic colitis, and pulmonary whatever-it-is. I get it. I'm still in my 30s, though, and I want to live a little. What good are all his millions if we can't shake our booties, eh?

I'd say things are getting worse. Mitch needs gallbladder surgery, a stent, and probably an operation for his spinal nerve problem. He takes a lot of medications. I think he's doped up, frankly. I try to pass the time with a few close friends. Richard takes me to the Shimmy Shack and we do some "heavy petting" in the car, which we both enjoy. Arnie invites me over to play "kissy-kissy." That always gets pretty wild. Ken shows me a good time, too, even though he isn't so great-looking naked.

I guess the real issue is whether my marriage can survive much longer. I hate that Mitch may never regain real "quality of life." Is it unethical to hide his meds from the nurse? Do you think if I got a "ghost" gun and shot him in the head while he was sleeping, and pretended a burglar did it, the police would believe me? What if I drown him in the bathtub? Can you recommend anyone who will "eliminate a problem" for cash?

—**Going Insane in Lake Champlain**

Dear Insane,

You should be careful. There's a fine line between mercifully ending a life—what the advocates call compassionate "euthanasia"—and murder with malice aforethought, which is probably illegal in your state. I generally adhere to a "live and let live" philosophy. Perhaps you could kick up your heels with Richard, Arnie, Ken, Joe Blow, John Doe, the Duke of Windsor, the Vienna Boys' Choir, the University of Vermont Marching Band, and whoever else tickles your fancy (or whatever they're tickling), and in ten or fifteen years (if not sooner) "the problem" will go away on its own.

Surely you understand that, as a responsible media columnist, I cannot advocate for "offing" your husband—rich and doddering though he may be. Should you truly wish to resolve matters by means of "euthanasia" (*wink, wink*), I have little doubt that you could troll the sleazy bars and dens of iniquity and dredge up a lowdown, sniveling rat who'd pull a trigger for you.

How things worked out:

After weighing Ms. Matrimony's advice, Going Insane decided not to purchase a ghost gun or hire a scumbum hitman. Instead, she knocked her husband down the stairs, making it appear as if the old geezer's motorized wheelchair had simply lost control. Free at last and heir to a $300 million estate, she took up with Arnie—who schemed to marry her and take the money, possibly by killing her.

These facts emerged primarily because Arnie was murdered first by a wildly jealous Richard, who, only weeks later, was shot in the head by jealous ex-convict Ken. Going Insane escaped justice but testified against Ken in his murder trial. She ultimately did go insane, landing in a mental ward, where she remains to this day. Her nephew Chris, a high school dropout, now lives on the estate and runs it.

Insults May Vary

So Many Women! Dating a Multiple Personality

The moment I say I'm dating a multiple personality, people tend to give me that creeped-out, say-what, bug-eyed look, as if there's something the matter with me. Far from it. Let me tell you, this type of arrangement has a few challenges—but many undeniable advantages. Imagine: I can (in effect) see three different women (or more!) in the same night, all for the price of a single date.

Take last Thursday, for instance. I was able to hit the Rusty Pelican with Evelyn (personality No. 1—the "main" or "primary" personality), who was her usual genial, rather aloof self as we chit-chatted about her domineering boss and dined on grilled salmon with asparagus spears and almond-crusted halibut in white-wine sauce. After that, I bellied up to the Hyatt bar with Beatrice (personality No. 6), a livelier woman who confided her dreams that I would whisk her away to Aruba. And then, incredibly, to close out the evening, I bedded down with Jocelyn (No. 9), a hot-blooded seductress who comes around about as often as the abominable snowman.

So much action—in a span of only six hours! Topping it off, the woman I know as Cecilia (No. 2) carped at me about watching too much sports on TV as I was flossing my teeth just before midnight.

Having entered this relationship—read: relationships—almost three years ago, I can now honestly declare: Of all the psychological disorders, this humdinger is easily the most fascinating.

Experts say a single individual may have up to fifteen distinct "selves." One personality may be right-handed, for example, while another—completely unaware of the first—is a lefty. One may spend prodigious amounts of money on high heels, pumps, skirts, leather handbags, diamond pendants, earrings, spa treatments, and other "necessities," while another may claim to be a frugal bargain-hunter with no idea any of it happened.

It took me about two weeks to realize Evelyn was not the only woman occupying the well-contoured body and pleasing countenance of the woman I met at my cousin's Labor Day party. In all, I have secretly documented ten wholly realized individuals and two of what I call "proto-personalities," meaning they could rear their ugly heads at any moment—and I go around in a semi-terrified state hoping to God they don't.

Before I go any further, let me interject a few caveats:

1. Evelyn has never been officially diagnosed.
2. So what? Would I need a zoologist's expert opinion to know a kangaroo if I saw one? I'll forgo the Park Avenue quack, thank you very much.
3. My life—which had been rather mundane and, dare I say, boring—has taken on the sort of bizarre unpredictability I've long admired in the works of Edgar Allan Poe and H.P. Lovecraft.
4. If I ever start screaming, I may never stop.

Here's a moment: We're touring the wine country, stopping at various vineyards, having a great time. The sun is out, and Evelyn looks nice in a simple white blouse and stone-washed jeans. I know it's Evelyn because she's pleasant and ethereal and likes to put a hand on my shoulder when we're talking close. We're side-by-side at a tasting counter, sampling a zinfandel with top notes and tannins and hints of balsa wood or ginkgo root or whatever the hell it has, and in walks this redhead in a halter top.

I swear I gave her no more than a glance.

Exit Evelyn. Enter Lorraine (No. 3), whose major personality feature—bless her heart—is that she can't stand anything that interferes with my fondest dreams and desires. Less than five minutes goes by and I hear Lorraine's voice sharp in my ear: "If you want to ask her out, I'll get lost and go pick grapes for a couple days."

"Grapes?" I say. "We can get those at Vons."

"Maybe you just want to fuck her," Lorraine adds, somewhat louder, as if to underscore her unbounded selfless generosity. "I'll see you back at the hotel tomorrow."

Unfortunately, as I've experienced over and over, Lorraine is the most transitory of the selves and never lingers for long. By the time we were back in the car, personality No. 8, Astrid, had taken over. Astrid is the brooding, silent type—she might even be mute—and must suffer a lingering neck injury, because I've never seen her turn her head to look at me. Not even once. Since we were touring in Evelyn's Nissan, I also got to observe that Astrid drives like the late stock car superstar Richard Petty. She'd be a scourge at Daytona if I could ever get her signed up.

Before that memorable evening was done, two other selves made an appearance: Cecilia, No. 10, who curses like the little Norwegian handyman who replaced my water heater; and Ruth (No. 4), who's still a virgin and always will be. Ruth, in fact, must have some acute inflammatory nerve disease—under no circumstances is she ever to be touched.

In my efforts to document and understand the many faces of Evelyn, I've kept notes, made charts, read books, and consulted with experts. At certain moments, I've even dared to ask her, point-blank: "Who are you?"—a question that invariably produces a non-response, often in the form of a whoa-wait-a-second counterattack. "Why, you've got some goddamn nerve, you self-centered dickhead!" That's how I recall Cecilia replying once—quite a contrast to how Astrid would've handled the same situation. Astrid excels at a blood-chilling glare. It generally lasts only an instant before she whirls on her heels, like a coked-up flamenco dancer, and exits without a word—only an ear-jarring slam of the door.

Now compare that to Lorraine—the sweet, ever-considerate

Lorraine—who attempts to defuse tensions by suggesting ways I can enjoy myself. "You want action tonight? Go find yourself a whore," she told me just last month. Another time it was, "Oh, you're a great guy, all right. Go fuck yourself."

I'd much rather encounter Lorraine than Maggie (proto-personality A), who once seized a torchiere lamp and tried to crack open my skull with it.

Diligent research has given me a well-rounded grasp of every player in this vexing chorus line. Here are a few notes I made concerning personality No. 7, Constance, whose judgmental nature is severe and unwavering: "By far the most intense watcher. Quick to rile and yet distinct from Cecilia and others mainly due to her emphatic use of hissing. 'You s-s-s-s-s-tupid, ins-s-s-s-sensitive ass-sssss!' she has said more than once. Speaks in low, snake-like tones. Possessed by demons?"

Personality No. 5, Pollyanna (I can name them anything I want), is a lot like Lorraine—and like Ruth, too, actually—except that she's obsessed with shopping. To be clear, personalities 1, 5, 7, 8, and 9 are also obsessed with shopping, and proto-personality B (Winifred) once bought a Sea-Doo on my charge card as revenge for some peccadillo of mine involving a woman named Carolyn, who is *not* part of the group.

In any event, Pollyanna's fixation is shoes—she's a modern-day Imelda Marcos—whereas Beatrice shops mainly for designer-name skirts, jackets, pants, and swimwear. Cecilia concentrates almost exclusively on pricey scarves, earrings, pendants, watches, and bracelets.

The net effect is a brimming closet—and a reliance on me to help pay for her groceries and electric bill. Evelyn herself, who refuses to spend money on clothes, gratefully accepts my largesse and freely borrows from the entire wardrobe.

It's a good bet she'll dip into that wardrobe tonight, because I've made reservations at Garamendi's—her favorite steakhouse—to celebrate her birthday. No doubt Evelyn will look fabulous, which is, of course, one reason I continue to date her. But the magic lies in the uncertainty. Which of the others will show up?

If I keep my eyes fixed closely enough on Evelyn, my martini glass, my porterhouse, and baked potato—ignoring every other female in the room—perhaps I can forestall the arrival of Lorraine or Astrid. The trickier task, though well worth attempting, will be to orchestrate every aspect of the evening—from the wine to the salted caramel ice cream to the pricey little trinket I will bestow on her later—so as to create for her the ultimate romantic experience.

If it works—if the night is a stupendous success—there's at least a smidgen of a chance that the elusive Jocelyn will slink her way through the bedroom door.

So far, no particular formula has proven reliable—her rare reappearances have a decided element of randomness—but when I see those eyes, that little dimpled smile, the bare contours of her shoulders in the candlelight, I feel a surge of joy and renewal. It's nice to know that Jocelyn is in there somewhere.

David Ferrell

A Farewell to Yarns: Drafts of My Resignation Letter from the Writers' Group

Dear Writers,
It is with great regret—

Dear Writers,
Regret fills me to the brim as I announce—

Dear East Valley Writers,
Very regretfully—

Dear Writers,
Every story has an ending (except for some of Lisa's), and, unfortunately, so too does my long involvement with the East Valley Writers Group. I regret that last week's meeting will have to be my last. While it pains me to leave on a sour note—

Dear Writers,
Every story has an ending, and sadly, so does my long involvement with the East Valley Writers Group. Last week's meeting was my last. Deep in my aching heart beats a solemn pang of regret, for I vividly remember the happy, hopeful promise of our inception nine years ago. As some of you know, I've become

increasingly disturbed by the relentless, mean-spirited (of course I mean you, Derek!) critiques of my essays, short stories, and, most of all, the chapters of my latest novel. A chimp pecking randomly at a keyboard would likely get more positive feedback than—

Dear "Writers,"

Like a tragic tale told by Dickens, my long involvement with—

Dear "Writers,"

Like a long and dreadful disease—

Dear "writers,"

My long involvement with the East Valley Writers Group has been, in many ways, like a marriage.

Attention "writers":

Every story ends—some of them well, and some in a cacophony of rancor and dysfunction. Naturally, I allude now to last week's meeting at Rich's house. That's it for me with this so-called writers group. I'm done. *Finis.* Out of there.

I quit!

No sane man (or woman) would continue to waste a perfectly decent evening every goddamn month by subjecting himself to such toxic nit-picking and literary ignorance. I could ignore the minor annoyances of Tanya's warmed-over bean dip and Bob's honking laugh if you imbeciles could at least attempt to grasp the deeper themes and nuances that I'm exploring in my prose. However, you cannot. You pig-headed narcissists have no clue, and yet you attack like hyenas ripping apart a blood sausage. I hardly need remind anyone of Derek's comments concerning the chapter in my novel dealing with Ryan's botched gum-graft surgery. Obviously, Derek, you've never experienced—

David Ferrell

Writers Group:

It's time for me to begin a new chapter. Am I talking about *House of the Crescent Moon*? Or am I speaking more broadly about my writing career? Actually, both—because as of this very moment—

East Valley Writers:

Needless to say, I was not pleased by the gangland-style attack job committed upon—

Dearest Writers,

As a parting "gift," because I'm ending my affiliation with you jackasses, I'd like to rescind—and in some cases revise—a few of the supportive and constructive comments I've expressed to members of the group in recent months.

I'll start with Leslie. Leslie, I've been way too nice. Those avant-garde "experimental" stories you're writing are utterly baffling, and I can't imagine anybody wanting to read them. They suck. They're godawful. You're in a dead heat with seven other members of the group for the worst writer I've ever met.

Rich, you're a moron. Even if, as you appear to believe, the world is clamoring for a novel about CIA-trained talking dolphins, no publisher will buy yours. It's atrocious. Give up. Jam it all into a fireplace on some winter night.

Rose, you stink. By any other name, would your poetry be just as stinking rotten? Shakespeare would say *ab-so-fucking-lutely*.

Derek, what can I say? Your head is so far up your ass you can probably count the spots on your liver. If I never hear your whiny nasal voice again—

Dear Fuckheads,

I hate to be negative—generally I'm not a negative person—

Fuckheads:

I've been sickened lately—

"Writers":

Every story ends—some badly, it turns out. I'm sorry to say that such is the case with my involvement in the East Valley Writers Group. I am quitting this asinine—

E.V. Writers:

Every story ends—few as badly as the story of my involvement in the East Valley Writers Group. Surely no one will be surprised to receive this note announcing my—

EV Writers:

It is with great pleasure that I announce my resignation from the—

Dear Writers,

You won't believe the incredible good fortune that befell me yesterday when my agent called to announce that HarperCollins is offering a six-figure advance for *House of the Crescent Moon*, even though I have not yet finished a full draft. I had no idea the agency was even sending it out! Apparently, there was too much excitement over the manuscript to withhold it any longer. I wish I had taped the conversation. We laughed and talked for nearly an hour and then I took Julie out to celebrate at Chez Janelle.

It's hard to imagine that only last week the novel was being ripped apart by you vacuous nincompoops at our latest meeting! Regrettably, due to my need to focus on completing the manuscript, I will not be able to attend next month's meeting, nor, probably, any subsequent meetings after th—

David Ferrell

Dear Writers,

Spectacular news! My agent called late yesterday to say HarperCollins is offering a million-dollar advance for *House of the Crescent Moon*! *(This, even though I have not yet finished the latest draft!)* "It's going to be a blockbuster—they're sure of it," Mr. Spitzer told me. And of course I couldn't help but reflect on last week's bitterly toxic meeting. A million dollars! Who'd have guessed it listening to Derek and the rest of you idiots spouting criticism after—

Dear "writers,"

Oh . . . my . . . GOD!

A $10 million advance for *House of the Crescent Moon*!

Just got the news and I'm literally shaking. Ecstatic? Beyond words! I can't even speak! And now they're going nuts over movie rights! Yes—for this same novel that you people have mercilessly attacked from Day One. Imagine!

Naturally, I'm too busy now to maintain my longstanding membership in the East Valley Writers Group.

So . . .

Goodbye, Leslie.

Goodbye, Rose.

Goodbye, Bob.

Goodbye, Tanya.

Goodbye, Rich.

Goodbye, Brad.

Goodbye, Allison.

Goodbye, Lisa.

Goodbye, Derek, you twat.

Remember me well.

Fuck you all, assholes.

Fight Night in L.A.

RAY:

Good evening, ladies and gentlemen, and welcome to the Lyons Avenue Bar, scene of tonight's main event: a showdown for the ages—a chance encounter between Rick "The Ex" McAdams, the man who dated Barbara for ten solid months last year and even proclaimed to his beer buddies that he might marry her, and Mike "New Flame" Finley, a hotshot lawyer who now takes Barbara everywhere, including the opera just last month. *Volare*, I believe—and Finley's not even an opera fan. These two type-A hard-noses are meeting by utter coincidence—they don't have a clue—right here in this trendy downtown watering hole, a real favorite of stressed-out working stiffs. And to help call the action, here's my longtime sidekick, Bones Donaldson. Bones, it doesn't get any better than this.

BONES:

No, it really doesn't, Ray. I'm thrilled to be here and can't wait to see how this debacle plays out.

RAY:

We shouldn't have to wait long. McAdams, who's had a tough run of luck since hitting on Barbara's yoga instructor, certainly has his game face on. He's planted himself at the end of the bar and appears to be drinking a Manhattan, straight up.

BONES:

Look at that intensity. You know, hitting on Allison was a huge mistake for him, Ray. He lost the relationship and now he's dating a Guatemalan woman who barely speaks English. That's his second Manhattan, and he'll be there a while—he just ordered chicken wings.

RAY:

The Cajun wings, a very popular item here, Bones. And meanwhile, here comes Finley, pushing past the crowd at the front door. He's due to meet Barbara here at seven, so he won't be chased off by the sight of his adversary, that's for sure. And there he goes—advancing toward the bar with those quick, mincing steps of his. Looks every bit the querulous lawyer. Scowling, tight-lipped.

BONES:

Happy hour, Ray, but that's a misnomer. Neither one of these—

RAY:

Excuse me, Bones—there it is! The first moment of recognition! They've just seen each other! Finley reached the bar not ten feet from McAdams and threw him a look—an absolutely mortified look that's now—

BONES:

It's hostile, Ray. No mistaking it!

RAY:

I don't think he realized McAdams was there! He had no idea until—oh, my God, how awkward!

BONES:

That's a hostile look, Ray!

RAY:

And McAdams, he's giving it right back. Staring like a man who's just seen a six-foot wharf rat—wearing Brooks Brothers!

BONES:

Glaring, Ray. Both just glaring at each other for a second there.

RAY:

Right! Yes! And now Finley's trying to go about his business, showing absolute indifference—as if such a thing were even possible.

BONES:

Neither one's going to move, Ray. Two tough, stubborn customers.

RAY:

They're—what? Seven, eight feet apart?

BONES:

Far too close for comfort, Ray. Exactly what we'd hoped for!

RAY:

Look at Finley now—reaching for the little drink menu there on the bar, scanning it. Staring at all those exotic cocktails.

BONES:

He prides himself on being cool. It's a side of him that Barbara really—

RAY:

And look at McAdams! There, Bones—did you see it? A sidelong glance! One long sidelong glance at Finley, and he's back to brooding over that Manhattan. Look at the body language!

BONES:

These two aren't friends.

RAY:

Oh, that's an understatement, Bones! Finley now trying to get the bartender's attention. New Flame is leaning well over the bar, deliberately ignoring McAdams, and now—yes!—a hard stare! Quite a hard stare for just an instant.

Where's that bartender? Okay, I think he sees him now. Any chance he'll go with one of those specialty drinks, Bones? An apple martini?

BONES:

Not in a million years, Ray. That menu's just for show. He'll go with one of his old stand-bys, in my opinion. A gin and tonic or a house margarita.

RAY:

He's been ordering that lately.

BONES:

He won't dare let The Ex see him order anything fruity. I'd be shocked.

RAY:

The bartender now advances toward him, moving along the bar. Tall fellow, kind of looks like Hugh Laurie. Long face. Let's listen in for a moment.

"Just a Bud Light. No, second thought—got any Mexican beers on tap?"

"Pacifico. Dos Equis. Corona."

"Dos Equis sounds good. And the mushroom caps."

"Amber or dark?"

"Amber. And another napkin."

RAY:

He goes for a Dos Equis, Bones!

BONES:

Dos Equis Amber, Ray! And mushroom caps! Those are—

RAY:

And Finley gives another long sidelong glance at McAdams. He practically taunted him that time! And McAdams looks back—eye-to-eye for an instant! They were locked up, Bones! Eye-to-eye!

BONES:

They might speak, Ray.

RAY:

I thought Finley wanted to say something. I really did.

BONES:

They're working themselves toward it. Those mushroom caps—

RAY:

Finley now looking around, waiting for his beer.

BONES:

He went with the Mexican beer, Ray. He balked a bit—looked tentative—but went with the Mexican beer and the $14 mushroom caps. There's certainly a message there. Those mushroom caps.

RAY:

He can afford Barbara—that's the message. He's the New Flame, and he's in charge. He's not afraid of ordering the $14 mushroom caps, even though—well, they're said to be good here, but they don't give you very much. Just four of them.

BONES:

Cheese-filled. Sharp cheddar.

RAY:

He had to get that across—Finley. Made his point and now—oh, look at him. Look at both of them! Another couple of glances. McAdams glaring now.

BONES:

I think he'll say something. I think The Ex may be the first to—

McADAMS:

"Strange you'd wander in here. Not stalking me, I hope."

RAY:

There it is! There it is! A comment!

BONES:

"Not stalking me"!

FINLEY:

"Stalking you? Oh my God."

RAY:

Finley comes back with that! Rolls his eyes! Look at him there, Bones—disgusted. New Flame is absolutely disgusted.

BONES:

McAdams too. McAdams is disgusted just looking at—

RAY:

A lot of anger in that man!

McADAMS:

"What? Why the look?"

BONES:

Another jab by McAdams! A jab and that surly glare!

FINLEY:

"My God, you don't have a clue. Stalking you?"

McADAMS:

"It was a joke. A joke, all right?"

RAY:

Back and forth! Look at them, Bones!

FINLEY:

"Oh, ha-ha. Yeah, a joke. You're a real comic."

McADAMS:

"I'm no tight-ass lawyer."

RAY:

Two zingers, Bones! Those stinging jabs remind me of Ali and Frazier! Tyson Fury the way he—

BONES:

Hard-hitting! Intense action!

FINLEY:

"Jesus. You're so damn clever. Ought to book yourself doing stand-up."

Insults May Vary

RAY:

Oh my God, what a counter! Finley takes his beer from the bartender now. He's pleased with that last remark—you can see it on his face. Takes his beer, swigs it, and there's another sidelong glance at McAdams—and The Ex—oh, he continues to look very angry, Bones.

BONES:

McAdams started to reply and stopped himself, Ray. A sign of—oh, now he's—

McADAMS:

"Barb thought I was pretty damn funny."

RAY:

Invoking the ex!

BONES:

The Ex invokes the ex!

FINLEY:

"Oh, did she?"

RAY:

Finley seems thrown here! New Flame is—

BONES:

Yeah, but that's a huge risk for McAdams, invoking the ex!

FINLEY:

"She didn't think it was very funny when you cheated on her."

RAY:

Oh, there's a huge haymaker, Bones! Huge!

McADAMS:

"Cheated on her? Cheated on her?"

RAY:

Listen to McAdams now! Listen to that tone of voice!

McADAMS:

"I had coffee with her yoga teacher! Coffee!"

FINLEY:

"Behind her back."

McADAMS:

"It was coffee, dude. And none of your business, a-hole."

RAY:

Look at that, Bones! Look at the righteous anger and regret etched on McAdams' face—and now he goes for that Manhattan. A big sip!

BONES:

New Flame stung him, Ray. McAdams opened himself up invoking the ex. One of the cardinal rules in this game—

RAY:

Excuse me, Bones, there at the front door—

BONES:

Speaking of the ex!

RAY:

There's Barbara just inside the front door, early for once. Looking nice, too. Wearing that—what do you call that, Bones?

BONES:

A classy look. Professional attire. Knee-length black skirt. Nordstrom, maybe. She's a college administrator—Parkland Institute, as we all know. Black pumps.

RAY:

Classy and—let's be honest—a hot number. No surprise she's looking good. And she's moving toward the bar. Due to meet New Flame here.

BONES:

Just in time for those mushroom caps. They'll be coming up.

RAY:

And McAdams is facing a decision now. He's drained his Manhattan and—there they are—the chicken wings. He got his appetizer first. So does he grab another drink here? He doesn't realize—

BONES:

Now he does, Ray! I think he's seen her!

RAY:

You're right, Bones! He just looked over and saw Barbara. Just saw—oh, look at his face now! Look at that expression!

BONES:

And look at hers, Ray!

RAY:

The edge clearly swings to New Flame. Finley's got a decided—

BONES:

A huge advantage, Ray!

RAY:

And Barbara comes in—right between them, Bones! She's right between them at the bar! Her eyes swing now toward The Ex. Eye contact here—and she isn't pleased!

BONES:

No, no she isn't! Let's listen to what she—

BARBARA:

"This is, what? Some happenstance? You're not stalking me, Rick, because if you are—"

McADAMS:

"Hell no, I'm not stalking you!"

RAY:

Barbara dives right in, suggesting that McAdams might be stalking her!

BARBARA:

"If you are, I'll call the police!"

BONES:

The police! She's not here a minute and—

McADAMS:

"Hey. Hey! I'm just here having a drink. Okay? I've been here an hour! Like I should know you two would show up?"

RAY:

McAdams scores on the reply! A good, strong reply. He raises his hands like he's saying, *Hey, I'm innocent.* He couldn't possibly have stalked her, Bones!

BONES:

Right you are, Ray. What a reversal. First McAdams accuses Finley of stalking and—

RAY:

And now the ex is raising the question about The Ex!

BONES:

Ferocious action here!

RAY:

Back and forth, like Tyson and Holyfield—but McAdams appears to be in big trouble. He's reeling. Hard to see how he could possibly win it.

BONES:

He's staring at those wings, Ray. He'd gladly have a few if circumstances were different.

RAY:

Barbara's leaning close to New Flame now. Let's listen to what—

BARBARA:

"Can we grab a table? Or go to Jimmy's?"

RAY:

The Ex heard that! He heard it.

BONES:

She wasn't whispering, Ray.

RAY:

Look at McAdams now—standing. I think he might be leaving, Bones! Standing and reaching for his wallet. Stabs Finley with another glare—

BONES:

That might've been for Barbara, Ray.

RAY:

—and throws a couple of twenties on the bar. Right next to those uneaten wings!

McADAMS:

"I've got better things to do."

BONES:

Oh, a bitter remark! Bitter!

BARBARA:

"Yeah, go practice your yoga."

RAY:

Barbara—lightning quick with the answer! A fast response, and lots of bitter sarcasm, Bones. And it's over! It is *OVER*! There goes McAdams, leaving the bar. He's not even waiting for change. He's a beaten man, Bones—soundly defeated before this capacity crowd.

BONES:

He left a $12 tip, Ray—and not because he really wanted to.

RAY:

He was that desperate. That eager to get the hell out after the brutal pounding he absorbed.

BONES:

Brutal, yes. And I'm sure there will be critics asking if this was a fair contest, Ray, given Barbara's fluke appearance and the difference she made at the end.

RAY:

Can you really call it a fluke? When she and New Flame see each other nearly every night?

BONES:

The fact is, McAdams showed early signs of holding his own. He was the aggressor early, when it was just him and Finley.

RAY:

True. That's true, Bones. There will be controversy after this one. We'll get into that and recap the scoring—after this brief word from our sponsors.

Acknowledgements

The author is grateful for the unyielding guidance and support of gifted writer friends—i.e., the Allegores and their ilk, who selflessly disregarded fatigue and eye strain to help make this book what it is. Among those deserving specific mention:

Orman Day
William D'Urso
Alina Ferrell
Sandra Sloss Giedeman
The Goblin Queen
Martin Miller
and the late, talented Jean Hastings Ardell
and Anne McAndrews

Author Bio

David Ferrell's dark-comedy baseball novel, *Screwball*, was optioned by Universal Pictures and featured by the Book-of-the-Month Club. Ferrell is a former staff writer at the *Los Angeles Times*, where he was a member of two Pulitzer Prize-winning news teams. Known for his sharp and lyrical writing style, he roamed the city from the trash-strewn streets of Skid Row to the palm-shrouded mansions of Beverly Hills. He wrote about homelessness, wealth, jailhouse violence, and extreme sports. His gripping coverage of the Badwater Ultramarathon was published in the anthology *Best American Sports Writing*. Ferrell and his family live in Long Beach, California.

www.ingramcontent.com/pod-product-compliance
Lightning Source LLC
Chambersburg PA
CBHW041301240426
43661CB00010B/983